BROKEN

A Journey of Grace

Julie G. Kennedy

ISBN 978-1-0980-9446-1 (paperback)
ISBN 978-1-0980-9447-8 (digital)

Christian Faith Publishing, Inc.
832 Park Avenue
Meadville, PA 16335
www.christianfaithpublishing.com

Unless otherwise noted, all Scripture quotations are from the King James Version of the Bible

Printed in the United States of America

This book is dedicated to the glory of God. I am thankful for all the family, friends, and ministries that prayed for my healing. I pray the Lord's rich blessing on their lives.

Contents

To me, who am less than the least of all
the saints, this grace was given.

—Ephesians 3:8

Blows that hurt cleanse away evil, As do
stripes the inner depths of the heart.

—Proverbs 20:30

And when I see the blood, I will pass over you…

—Exodus 12:13b

Preface

B reaking news: it is meant to grab our attention.

Have you ever been interrupted by news, a tweet, Facebook message, phone call, or a knock at the door that just grabbed your attention or disrupted your life?

For me, it was a game changer. It was the news that came out of the blue. It caught me off guard and shook me to the core. I didn't know what to do. I thought everything was going my way: sunny days and a bright future. But then, suddenly, my life came to a screeching halt.

It was surreal. It was a huge time-out. I questioned who was calling the shots? Who blew the whistle? What in the world? I just wasn't ready for this and didn't have time to deal with it either.

Suddenly, I was face to face with an opponent that I didn't know how to handle. I felt unprepared. There was no time to ask why? It just wasn't supposed to happen this way. I was supposed to live happily ever after. I thought I had everything planned out. But this changed everything.

Are the things we consider disruptive meant to drive us to our knees, change our focus, redirect our path? Are the breaking points in life actually divine appointments that God uses to grab our attention? Are they pivotal and defining moments?

See, there is a time and season for everything under His sun. God either allows, arranges, or appoints the times in our life. It is a hard thing to be broken. It is hard to humble ourselves under the mighty hand of God. Actually it is a fearful thing to fall into the hands of God.

But we don't always get to choose. And I knew better than to shake my fist at God. After the initial shock, I called my family and we all gathered around and prayed.

Soon I understood the why? God broke me gracefully. It was God's will and the trigger prayer that set God in motion and put me on the Potter's wheel, the great anvil of His grace and in the fiery furnace of His great love.

Everyone has experienced breaking points in life's journey—disappointments, tragedies, or heartaches. What has left you shattered, compromised your beliefs, challenged or jeopardized your existence? Without Him, I would forever be broken, obscured, flawed, useless, and hopeless. But then I realized that He gracefully broke me and gracefully put me back together.

I hope that my story will encourage you to surrender to Him, give Him your brokenness and allow Him to put the pieces of your life back together His way. Come with me, I invite you to take time out and sit with me, for just a little while, and see God's grace in taking the broken and making something beautiful from it.

Introduction

Their backs were against the wall. Remember Exodus 14, the story about the deliverance of the Israelites? They had seen God's miracles in Egypt. God was in their midst and He was in the process of delivering them from the wicked ruler. But just when they thought they were home free and so close to the promised land, they hit a dead end. They could see the promised land but couldn't get to it. Then things got even worse. When they looked back they saw the billowing cloud of dust rising from the chariots and horses. They heard the clanking of the swords, spears, armor and the cracks of the whips driving the horses faster toward them. Frantically they looked for a way of escape but seeing that they were cornered between the side of a mountain and the Red Sea, they lost hope. They were trapped.

In anger, despair, and frustration they turned to Moses. He beseeched God. It was eleven fifty-nine. No time to spare. And then God made a way. He made a way of escape from looming and seemingly eminent disaster. Just when the walls of death were fast closing in around them and they didn't understand the trouble encompassing them, God had a plan of salvation already worked out. He did have everything under His control. But they were scared out of their right mind. In the heat of the battle, their consciousness of God lapsed, and they forgot how the angel of God kept them safe from the enemy while they were in the desert. Remember how He guided them with a cloud by day and a pillar of fire by night? Remember all the miracles in Egypt God performed in their midst? How could they forget His salvation, grace, shepherding and love for them through all those times? Their deliverance was going to be from Him and in His time and in His way. He was dramatically going to change their lives, defeat their enemies before their very eyes, and forever be remembered in time. It was for their good and for His glory. With this story and many other stories of God's salvation, deliverance, and healing, I went on in faith believing, waiting on Him and trusting Him with my life as I hope you do too.

He heard me. He saw my condition and knew about it before I did. Also, He heard the intercession of His people. He brought my husband, Mike from death to life after a bad motorcycle accident, healed him from many injuries and helped him to overcome many other challenges. He answered many prayers and brought a wayward son home and back to Himself. He heard me and saved me from many other troubles. Our voices He heard in Heaven. He moved with compassion. He was working through a condition in me for my good and His glory. It has been for His glory. Somehow, He seemed to bow the Heavens and came to even me. Miraculously, through His Spirit and through His Word, He has touched my life. Now I have a testimony to share, lengthy, yes, but extraordinary. He answered so many prayers on my behalf and heard my cry for mercy and He moved upon my life. I am so amazed that I was salvageable and redeemable, not just for eternity but for extension and preservation of my life here on earth, to tell you a story about Him. You see, He is the Master Storyteller.

He indeed took me, a "whosoever" according to John 3:16, forgave me, healed me and gave me a horn to raise, a testimony of His great love. Hopefully something I share in my story will give you hope to believe in Him. Let Him use your trials, circumstances or situation to become your story of His grace and His mercy that endures forever. I hope that according to Ephesians 1:18–19, "that ye may know what is the exceeding greatness of His power to us-ward who believe," and according to Ephesians 2:6, that "we are His workmanship," and according to Ephesians 3:18–19, that you "may be able to comprehend with all the saints what is the breadth, and the length, and the depth, and height; and to know the love of Christ."

Romans 1:17 says, "For in it the righteousness of God is revealed from faith to faith; as it is written, 'The just shall live by faith.'"

Psalm 119:14, 22, and 24 says,

> I have rejoiced in the way of Thy testimonies, as much as in all riches.
>
> Remove from me reproach and contempt, for I have kept Your testimonies.
>
> Thy testimonies also are my delight and my counselors.

Hebrews 11:1–2 says, "Now faith is the substance of things hoped for, the evidence of things not seen. For by it the elders obtained a good report."

This is my testimony of Him, a good report of His work through my journey of His grace; from being broken to being restored, whole, and now fashioned for the Master's use.

The Checkup

Wednesday, May 23. I went for a wellness checkup. The next day, the physician's assistant called me in and told me that everything looked fine except for an unusually high white blood cell count. Sixty-one was the count. Ten was the high end of normal. But I shrugged my shoulders and nonchalantly questioned what the big deal was and what the high numbers meant anyway. As she grabbed her chart, she looked at me and told me that it was Leukemia.

Instantly a cold chill went down my spine. But my knee jerk reaction was denial, "well, whatever," and dismissed her response, thinking she was way off the radar. She was just a physician's assistant. I hadn't been too impressed with her before, so I kind of brushed off her answer. I reasoned that there must have been a typo in the results. Since everyone makes mistakes, I requested that another test be done.

The Call That Changed My Life

F riday, May 25. I went in for another blood test. I had known the nurse who took the blood test for years. She just shook her head and said, "You just never know." I didn't like that response from her. As I was checking out, I told the office staff that they didn't need to call me if everything was ok. But, if there was a problem, I requested that the doctor of the practice call me back. The next day, Saturday morning, I hadn't gotten any calls and I knew that my doctor's office had closed at noon. I had just breathed a sigh of relief when the phone rang. I reluctantly looked at the identity of the incoming call. It was my doctor. It was the call that changed my life. The news that no one wanted to hear. He recommended that I see a hematologist as soon as possible because the white blood cell count had risen higher, to sixty-five. Although I really didn't want to hear his answer, I asked him what he thought. He told me the only time he saw numbers that high is in people who have Leukemia. I was scared. But he told me that there was a lot they could do if I got treatment immediately.

The possibility of a life-threatening condition made the Memorial Day weekend that much more somber. I always like to hope for the best, but plan for the worst. Mike and I spent the rest of the weekend discussing funeral arrangements. He was very upset. I could hardly even pray. We were just in shock.

Jesus, the Blood Expert

— ◦ —

Tuesday, May 29. After the long Holiday weekend, my physician sent his lab results to the hematologist. Shortly thereafter, the hematologist's office called and told me to be in the office on Wednesday morning, the next day.

At that point, I turned to Jesus, THE chief hematologist, the blood expert, and brought the condition of my blood to Him. Right, where else do you go? I believe that there is power in His blood that covers me.

Buying Time

Wednesday, May 30. My husband, Mike, and my oldest son, drove me to the appointment to see the hematologist. As we drove up to the address, there was a big sign on the building indicating that it was a cancer center. I thought there must have been some kind of mistake. We must have taken a wrong turn. I was scheduled to go to a hematologist, not a cancer center. But the address was correct. When I walked in it was as quiet, clean, and as sterile as a morgue.

As I slowly and hesitantly walked toward the front desk, I saw a lady through the big fish tank rolling her chair to the front desk. She was just as nice as she could be. But I didn't like all the paperwork I had to sign and I wasn't comfortable with the way they assumed I was checking in for an extended stay. "What was I getting myself into here," I thought. But I played along with it. In the back of my mind I knew that my physician was usually right in his diagnosis. He is not an alarmist but recognizes what needs attention. Even though the people there were just so nice,

I was still about scared out of my mind. Halfway through the paper work, I thought about running out the door, but since I had gone this far, I reasoned sensibly and then thought: I might as well go through with the appointment and see what the doctor had to say. They ran their own tests. To my surprise and to their surprise, the white blood cell counts had risen well into the seventies, higher than the last test. I didn't freak out yet, but they moved fast so as not to let things get out of control. As this was all happening before my very eyes and in me, I just didn't understand it all. Where did this come from? Other than a recent dentist appointment I was fine, no pain other than a lingering soreness in my jaw from the shots that the dentist gave me. I had been tired lately but just figured that it was because of being busy and stressed out.

The hematologist/oncologist started explaining his plan of action. But first he explained my condition in a simile. He said that my condition is likened to a beautiful green lawn except for a few weeds popping up that need to be identified and taken out before they spread and ruined the whole lawn. As a gardener of the lawn, he would cut the whole lawn short which would stop the weed from growing until he could find out how to treat the weed. I looked at him and said, "The good with the bad" and he nodded his head. Then I asked him how short and he said, "Really short." I took a moment but could see he was anxious for me to agree. I realized the clock was ticking and as fast as things were moving, didn't have any other options at that point. There was no time to waste. I understood his thinking, trouble shooting skills and agreed with the plan of attack.

He said, "Great." It would buy him some time while he figured out what was causing the rapid rise of white blood cells and hopefully intervene with something to turn things around before it was eternally too late. He was pretty serious. His suspicion was that it was some form of Leukemia. I further sensed his urgency to move more aggressively. My last question was, "Is there hope?" His response bothered me. He just said, "Hope…" crossed his arms, thought about my question but didn't say anything else.

After we left the office we went straight over to the pharmacy which is only about a mile down the road. Surprisingly, when we got there the medicine, a few prescriptions, were ready. I was in a bit of dismay. Wait a minute, chemotherapy was for cancer patients. Wasn't this rather sudden. Could I trust this doctor? Should I get a second opinion? Questions were swirling through my mind. But there was no time to waste. The doctor explained that if they didn't stop the bad white blood cells from going higher, it could cause other problems. So my husband and I paid for the medicine, grabbed the bags and headed home where I could start the process.

I had heard and seen all the bad side effects of chemo-therapy. It was scary. The medicine is so toxic that no one else can even touch the bottle without gloves. So it came down to the old skull and cross bones. I thought it looked dangerous and wondered if it would kill me. Suddenly I felt so isolated. I had to quarantine myself from anyone until further notice. But if it would buy the doctor time to figure it out, then I really didn't have any other choice. Meanwhile, the doctor told me to rest up for the bone biopsy he scheduled for the next day. Since the bone mar-row is where the red blood cells, platelets, and white blood cells are generated and released in the body, he would need to get a biopsy of my bone marrow and have it examined to see what was going on.

Someone once told me how painful bone marrow biopsies could be. The doctor can numb the flesh around the bone but not numb the bone itself. He told me that extracting bone marrow is like trying to get a thick milk-shake out of a straw. Although I dreaded it, I knew there was no way out of it. The Lord reminded me of the pas-sion week, when He went down the road called, La Via Dolorosa. He set his face like flint to Jerusalem. He was determined to do what God had planned for Him. He had no pain killers, no one to hold His hand through His suf-fering, as they drove the nails through His hands and feet. He could relate to the dread of what was ahead of me. He promised me that He would never leave me and that His Holy Spirit would comfort me.

Jesus buys our time. There is no time to waste. Don't let sin creep in your life and eat away at your precious life.

God's Wake-Up Call

———— ✑ ————

Thursday, May 31. Mike gave me Psalms 57:1–3:

> Be merciful unto me, O God, be
> merciful unto me: for my soul trusteth in
> thee, yea, in the shadow of Your wings I
> will make my refuge until these calamities
> be overpast. I will cry out to God Most
> High, to God who performs all things for
> me. He shall send from heaven and save
> me. He reproaches the one who would
> swallow me up. God shall send forth His
> mercy and His strength.

The next morning another blood test was done that revealed a higher white blood cell count. The numbers had risen into the nineties, which oddly enough made the biopsy easier to endure. The pressure was on. It was a race against time. While the nurses and lab people were performing the procedure, the sharp deep pain made me think about the unbearable pain Jesus endured for us.

The Lord blessed me with a very loving Christian nurse who held my hand the whole time. She kept the conversation going during the approximately thirty minutes to distract my attention away from the procedure. After it was done, I was so relieved and so was the nurse. Well, it was over. The doctor got what he needed to figure out what was going on. They quickly whisked the biopsies off to a genetic lab for test analysis and demanded the process and results be expedited in order to make a definite diagnosis and in turn provide some options for the most effective treatment as soon as possible.

In the waiting, I was thanking the Lord that my mother and aunt put me on their church prayer lists in Florida. Glad too that my pastor called me and asked if I would like to be put on my church prayer list. I agreed and was just overwhelmed that so many Christians were praying for me. My mother also called a prominent ministry for prayer and they told her that they would continue praying for me. Word spread quickly. People were just dumbfounded because overall, I have been very healthy, eating well, and working out daily. I was so comforted that so many prayer groups were concerned and praying for me. Even one of my son's best friends, who claimed to be an Atheist was so moved with compassion, that he told Josh to tell me that he would be praying for me too. My oldest son, who was the most distraught, went to work. Upset, yes, but went to work anyway. He said everyone where he worked was coming up to him and giving him hugs and telling him that they would be praying for me. I am so thankful for people's hearts that had been touched and moved to pray for me. It overwhelmed me to know that so many people cared.

In the meanwhile, I humbly waited on the Lord and was thankful for everyone's prayers. Seeking the Lord like never before! Waiting on him. It was up to Him now.

A lot of things came to my mind, areas I needed to get right in. More than the physical crisis at hand, I had to take care of my business with God, meaning my relationship with the Lord in case my time was up. It was the wake-up call.

When I touched base with my medical doctor, he tried to reassure me that there was a lot out there to treat and possibly fix the problem. But I would not rest until the hematologist/oncologist got all his results since he was more on the worst-case scenario side and expressed a grimmer outlook. Actually, I was really scared and concerned. What in the world was going on? Seemed like one day and a test result would shake me to the core and turn my world upside down.

End of Life

$\mathcal{CD}$

Again, more than the physical challenge at hand, was that if I died soon, I wasn't ready to go before the Lord. There was and is so much that I still need to do. I hadn't even started living for Him and really done what the Lord had called me to do. Never done so much end-of-life thinking. Everyone will face death: end of life here on earth. Recently, I heard someone who was faced with just a few weeks to live, surprisingly relate that he had no regrets. I don't know about you, but I certainly would have had regrets if I died within a few weeks or months. The past is the past. However, we all have a purpose to fulfill with our short span of life, the dash between the dates. And if you are not about our Father's business, doing His will for your life, you will have regrets. Only Jesus has no regrets. We must stay focused and diligently complete the tasks that the Lord has given us to do.

My husband told me that you really can't start living until you learn how to deal with death. As Christians we are to die to ourselves and live for Christ. Truth is, according to Colossians 3:3: "For ye are dead, and your life is hid with Christ in God."

The other day, the Lord brought a message to my attention regarding the intense heat that gold goes through in the refining process of purification. Also, a diamond doesn't shine until it is cut, and lastly how light shines the brightest in the dark. I just knew God was going to use these analogies for what He was putting me through. In other words, God was preparing me for what was to come. Did I really ask for this? But it was becoming clear that God will do whatever it takes. Heat, cutting, a dark time might all be in God's plan to make me what He wants me to be.

A recent lesson I taught my kindergarten Sunday School class on the sovereignty of God challenged me to pray about that personally. I wanted to know God's sovereignty in my life. Around the same time, some other things had paralleled that prayer. The office drama and politics were wearing me down. It was getting old. I didn't like the way things had fallen over the last few years.

I prayed, beseeched the Lord, pleading with the Lord, hoping that if it wasn't too late, that in His sovereign way and power, He would move upon my life. I prayed that if I wasn't where He wanted me to be that He would get me to where He wanted me to be. Now, looking back, this must have been God's will and the trigger prayer setting in motion the beginning of a journey back to God. So like clay in the potter's hand, I willingly submitted myself as He began to mold and remake me into His image. I yielded to Him as He carefully aligned me on His anvil of grace. I trusted Him day by day through the refining process of His love.

How I missed the days of spending time in His presence and I wondered if I would ever get there again. Sometimes it's hard to see The Potter when you're on the wheel, but He was right there, shaping and molding me closer to His image. The full-time job outside the home really gets in the way of spending time with Him. I knew the Lord was using the workplace and people. I think he allowed the job all these years and has used me in the downtown area to be a Godly witness, but I don't believe the job was His perfect will for my life.

More than a vacation, I needed a reprieve or a time-out to seek God, to come to Him, my Fortress and Refuge, and whether I wanted to or not, to accept the coming changes.

The news that came out of the blue was not what I expected from the Lord. I didn't win a million dollars or inherit a million dollars to get me out. What came my way was an out of range test result and the diagnosis that seems all too common these days and what no one wants to hear: the "C" word. So, before I knew it, I was out of the office and whisked off from one appointment to another.

I remember reading Matthew 11:28–30, where Jesus said,

> "Come unto me, all ye that labor and are heavy laden, and I will give you rest. Take my yoke upon you and learn of me; for I am meek and lowly in heart: and ye shall find rest for your souls. For my yoke is easy, and my burden is light."

He reminded me that we who are weary, who labor and are heavy laden, could come to Him. That He would give us rest. In Him we would find rest for our souls. He also promised that His yoke would be easy and His burden light.

Deep down, under all the layers, façade, game face, I felt I would be totally undone if something didn't change. No amount of money is worth your soul.

My husband felt the same way. We needed to unload the stuff of life, live light, try to free ourselves from the entanglements of the world and pursue the things of the Lord rather than man's work, corporate America and service to the government which Mike and I find so often offends our faith and requires us to work in politically correct but morally incorrect environments.

The Driving Storm

As I further self-examined my status, my position and direction in life, I also realized that I had started sliding down the slippery slope of moral decay. My beliefs, values, and morals were deteriorating down to dangerous levels. It was critical. The waves of worldliness and ungodliness and the lies of the devil and twisted truths were about to drown me out as a Christian. I felt like a ship out in a stormy dark sea, lost without a compass, tossed and turned by the tumultuous raging sea. My life was lost in the sea of compromise. Likened to a ship taking in too much water crashing over the bow, unable to calm the raging seas, I felt like I was drowning. I needed a savior. At one point a ship is either going to sink under the weight of the water or get driven into the rocks, shipwrecked and break into a million pieces. If a ship veers too far off course it can lose sight of land. Even worse, with no compass and strong winds, stormy weather and currents pulling it away from shore, even the light of the lighthouse can be snuffed out by the incredible pitch black of the night. At the point of no return, no one, not even the Coast Guard can save a ship. Only God could save now.

It was like the worst storm came upon me and from within me. As I looked around at the outside influences I took an assessment of what was left inside to see what condition I was in to fight. I was weak and broken.

Have you ever seen those tall pines here in North Carolina sway in a storm? When the adverse winds blow hard they bend. But if the roots aren't strong and the ground around is soft, the whole tree can uproot. Trees have weak points too. Sometimes because of poor circulation or disease the life and moisture doesn't get to every part of a tree and when the wind blows really hard that weak point is where it breaks off. Likewise, I think that Christians can break at weak or dry points when the winds of ungodliness blow, ever-pressing them to bend, to compromise just a little more until "snap" and down they go. And if it wasn't for the grace of God none would be mended to rise up, grow again and give God the glory.

I realized the slow descent in my life. A little here and a little there. Compromise. I had started caving in, living below my calling. Drifting farther and farther away from the bold and courageous life, dropping below the radar as a silent Christian, slipping down into relativism, away from absolute truth. I wasn't the Godly testimony or light in the dark place anymore. My light was about to go out. Revelations crossed my mind. I remembered when Jesus warned one church that He would take away their lampstand if they didn't repent and get back to their first love—love for the Lord. Love the Lord with all your heart, strength, mind, and soul.

Reluctantly, I was on the verge of resigning myself to a life similar to the Israelites, enslaved to the Egyptians, their cruel task master. My days reminded me of God's people, our ancestors, who just spent their days in Egypt, carrying heavy burdens, stomping through the mud pits, even taking beatings for not making bricks for Pharaoh fast enough. Until, they cried out to God. He heard their cries and planned to deliver them. For me it was one of those silent prayers. But I even doubted if God would hear me because I felt I had gone too far, crossed too many lines, and it would take a miracle not to be closed off from Him. Would the love of God still forgive me and restore me? Could He find me? Would He rescue me? I wondered, and I waited on Him. I would not deserve it and had not earned it. I could only go before Him on my knees and ask for mercy.

God reminded me of something that happened years ago. It was something that happened to me which helped me believe in Him. The Lord reminded me of what He did and that helped me hold on to my faith in Jesus, to find me, save me, and rescue me. After a five-and-a-half-hour surgery, part of me came to from the anesthesia. I was in a dark hole in the ground. Some part of me, not my body, maybe my soul was at the bottom. The ground and the walls around me were all fresh dirt. I wondered how I would ever get out. There was no rope, no ladder and I didn't even have a body to work with. Then I looked up for a way out. Way up I could see a hole with light. A nurse was calling me, I heard her, but I didn't know how to get to her. I was scared out of my mind. Was I going to live like that forever? So I prayed, and asked God if He would get me out of the hole, then I would live for Him. Instantly, I was on a gurney in the recovery room. I was so thankful that God heard my prayers and raised me up out of that dark cold place. Only God could have done that miracle. God had done His part, but I had not kept up my end of the deal. I hoped there was still time for me to do what I promised Him years ago. I remembered what the Lord had done. In faith, I prayed and waited for the Lord. I knew nothing would be impossible for Him and I also knew only God could heal me. I knew that His grace was greater than my need and it is greater than your need too.

Solemn Silence

———— ⌘ ————

F riday, June 1. I woke up to a Christian radio station. My alarm is set to 4:15 a.m. which is early, but it gives me time to get ready for the day. My routine of prayer, Bible reading or listening to a message, taking care of the dogs, exercising, deciding on an outfit for the day and making my meals for the day all take time. I couldn't help but listen to this pastor express so much passion and emotion about how God's riches can provide for whatever is before us that we are facing. You could sense a solemn silence and pause between and amidst his words. That was the Lord.

The Bridge of Prayer

G od brought my attention to another message urging us to get serious in prayer for America. God has
already used this condition to get me back to intercessory
prayer, to earnest help me Jesus prayer. Second Corinthians
4:16–18 encourages us not to lose heart that even as our
outward man is perishing, our inward man is being renewed
day by day and our relatively light affliction is working in
us a far more exceeding eternal glory. The things we see are
temporary and the things we can't see are eternal. The thing
that bridges the gap is prayer. Our future and the difference
between life and death teeter on our prayers.

Later on that day, I happened to listen to a pastor share
a story about a time he took his daughter out to celebrate
something she had achieved and told her she could have
anything she wanted. Rather than look for a dress on sale
she went to a jewelry store and asked to see a ring that
she had her eye on. The salesman pulled out a black velvet
cloth, laid it down on the glass counter under the light
and then placed the ring on the black cloth. The black

cloth enhanced the sparkle of the ring. It brought out the contrast between the dark cloth and the gem and the light and the brilliance of the gem. The black backdrop drew the attention to the piece of jewelry that was on display. Likewise, the Lord asks us to lay our lives down for him to place us where He wants us to be. Remember the prayer, "Lord, send me?" Perhaps it will be in a circumstance that is likened to a black, dark velvet cloth on top of a clear transparent surface, placed under the light for us to shine and display the Glory of God and His handiwork. Just like light penetrates a gem, so that the gem refracts and reflects the light, brilliant in all angles, that might be just what the Lord wants to do with our lives. He can make surfaces before unnoticed come to light for His glory.

Embedded Sins

A friend and sister in the Lord of my aunt called me from Chicago. She started a prayer ministry and outreach over forty years ago. It has grown and is still thriving and involved in planting churches in and around the Chicago area as well as other states. Aside from many important official positions she has in City and State government, she still serves the Lord, the people of Chicago, and surrounding areas. I was honored and excited that she took time to call me and talk to me. We got to sharing several things. She emphasized embedded sins. The message she shared with me made me go deeper in my soul searching. When I realized that I didn't even know how to search my own soul, the Holy Spirit reminded me of Psalm 139:23–24, "Search me, O God, and know my heart: try me, and know my thought: And see if there be any wicked way in me and lead me in the way everlasting."

Only the Word of God, conviction of the Holy Spirit and confession can cleanse us from those deep embedded sins. Thankfully, according to John 1:9, "If we confess our sin God is faithful to cleanse us from all unrighteousness."

God forbid we take one more breath or take one more step as a flawed, ineffective or defective Christian. My husband, the IT "guru" said that hackers embed viruses and bad code into good code. Think about that. Sin to a Christian can be like bad code in a computer. Both seek to destroy. So we need to be serious and diligent. We need to keep God's Word in our hearts. According to Psalm 119:11, "Thy Word have I hid in mine heart, that I might not sin against God."

We need to allow His Word and His Holy Spirit to be that search light of our soul.

When we can't see the way forward, allow God's Holy Spirit to search us and show us the way.

Also, ask God to rule in our hearts and minds through Christ Jesus.

The other day the doctor explained that the term Leukemia is a way of describing a blood disorder. Maybe Christians that have something wrong in their makeup are like that. But I do believe and know that the blood of Jesus cleanses us and makes us whole and functional. For me and my life, what God used in my life is my health. Now it is pivotal and contingent on staying right with the Lord, confessing my sin and not offending Him and His work. As a warning from a sister in Christ—whatever it is He uses to humble you under His hand, submit to His Sovereign move, and whatever He uses to accomplish His purpose in your life. He can use us or bench us or take us out of the game. If we don't abide in Him and Him in us we can get to a point where we become dysfunctional. So we need to stay right with Him, renounce unacceptable behavior, and respect what the Lord has done. Do not give Him the cold shoulder or shirk off His leading or quench His Holy Spirit. Keep short accounts with God, yield to Him, and obey His leading.

Before all this happened, I had drifted so far from where I was supposed to be, as I explained earlier. I knew it, deep down inside. My behavior and attitude, what was inside of me was wrong and needed to be corrected and made right, but I kept it hidden.

The last several years I found myself at times going along with almost twisting or compromising the truth to accommodate co-workers, hoping it would get me ahead. I almost got to the point where sin was understandable and justifiable. I tolerated their sin just to get along with them and gave up on praying for them.

We should never, never, never compromise the truth. It would be better to get fired over our convictions. Deep down, I wondered if my sin had caused a literal dysfunction in my blood or a twisted disordered chromosome that affected my blood cells. Serious alright. I was still hoping that the Lord's blood would cleanse that embedded sin. Hopefully He will fix what I allowed sin to break and straighten me out. I was and am looking for His mercy.

Similar to the process of purifying precious metals, deep embedded sins, like the impurities in the metal, are only brought up or out when the heat is turned up or it is placed in a fiery furnace. Has He heard me? Has He picked me up and put me through a scourging process out of His great love? Is this condition my fiery furnace? Maybe, yes. I know He is good all the time and all the time He is good. I believe the Lord is using this to prepare me, cleanse me, and purge me from sin. Only when the heat is turned up and the pressure is on do we get serious. Right, only when the gun is held to our head or our arm is twisted do we tell the truth and hope for mercy.

A line in a Christian movie summed it up as "reconcile the actions of your life before it's too late." Faced with this life-threating disease, I really did a lot of getting right, repentance and trusting God for him to heal me spiritually and physically and get me right with Him, right down to the cellular building blocks (the micro-cellular level)—DNA and bone marrow. God's purification process is thorough and complete.

Today another very special thing happened to me. This morning God was calling me to His Word, His Holy

Scriptures. I felt Him leading me in my spirit. After taking care of a few things around the house I pulled myself away from the earthly things and I finally got up to my study to settle myself before Him. When I got upstairs the blinds were not opened yet, but the sun was so strong. The rays were just penetrating through every crack, like it could not be held back. It was about to burst into the room. Just so bright and yet the full force and blast of light would not come in unless I opened the blind. It was almost like a blinding light. It was unusually strong. Then I opened the blind. Light flooded the room. The light overcame the dark. We have a choice to stay in the dark or turn to and open-up to the light and let it in our lives. John 1:4–5a says, "In Him was life; and the life was the light of men. And the light shines in the darkness…" and John 8:12 says, "Then spake Jesus unto them saying, 'I am the light of the world: he that followeth Me shall not walk in darkness, but have the light of life.'"

The light was soothing because of the dark prognosis from the doctor. The light seemed to overcome the darkness that was suddenly trying to overshadow me and pull me down into an early grave. Jesus is the Light. He brings light and life as we allow Him into our lives. Light overcomes darkness.

Live or Die

―――――― ⌘ ――――――

Did I have to decide whether to live or die or was it God that would decide that? I wasn't sure. I definitely wanted to live, but live by faith and not just live to go back into the same old grind. Living without God isn't worth it. Then I felt His strong presence, like I used to. I told the Lord that I had so missed Him all these past years. He was all I ever wanted. How I missed Him. Then I thought about heaven. I hadn't gotten a final word from God on how to take this.

I have always thought that when I die, the first people I want to look for in heaven are my grandmother and my Dad and then my favorite puppy dog. So I pulled up a chair I have that is special to me. It was my grandmother's kitchen chair that I got from her when she lived in Utrecht, The Netherlands. It is very special. I never allow anyone to sit in it. Only my memory of her. I thought, wouldn't it be nice if she was sitting there and we could talk, and she could tell me what heaven is like. Then it was as if I could see her just so happy and rejoicing, like she looked forward to my homecoming, whenever that would be. I lay down on the couch my Aunt gave me. My aunt bought it when she lived in Chicago years ago to accommodate my 6' 4" Dad when he visited her and my mother. My Dad always said, "Do you follow me?" I thought, sure, I follow you. See, I really didn't know how much longer I had to live. Maybe today would be the day I would follow them in heaven. As I gazed out the window, I thought about how grand heaven will be. Then, it was as if I couldn't even feel my body. I was in so much peace. I felt so comforted at the thought of my Grandmother sitting in that chair and laying on the same couch that my Dad rested on. It was so peaceful. I could have slipped away or stayed there. At that moment, I even thought that I would like to be laid to rest right on that couch rather that in a coffin. All my fears of death were gone. I thought of the verse in 1 Corinthians 15:55–57: "O death, where is thy sting? O grave, where is thy victory? But thanks be to God which giveth us the victory through our Lord Jesus Christ."

Death has no power over us. Then I realized I was still on the couch. My two dogs were so peaceful lying on the floor right next to me. Then I got up and sat down in my chair and started praying very intensely. The presence of the Lord was so very strong, and I was just waiting on Him. Then Psalm 71:14–16 came to me, which says,

> "But I will hope continually" (that was something the doctor didn't give me) "and will yet praise Thee more and more. My mouth shall shew forth thy righteousness and Thy salvation all the day; for I do not know the numbers thereof. I will go on in the strength of the Lord GOD: I will make mention of Thy righteousness, even of thine only."

So that was His word for me. It was and is so living and active and powerful. I received it. He was going to save and deliver me.

My next thought turned to the chemotherapy treatments I had already started and the upcoming appointments. Again, I looked to the Lord for direction on what to do about all those treatments. God's Spirit heavily impressed upon me Isaiah 41:10 which says, "Fear thou not; for I am with thee: be not dismayed for I am thy God: I will strengthen thee: yea, I will help thee: yea, I will uphold thee with the right hand of my righteousness."

I was so overcome with His strong presence, and His Words of life to me, to trust Him through the upcoming days.

Deuteronomy 8:3 says, "So He humbled thee…that He might make thee know that man doth not live by bread only, but by every word that proceedeth out of the mouth of the LORD doth man live."

I got up and was so relieved and at peace with whatever He would have for me whether it was in the grave or to stay here. He had extinguished my fears.

I had to get ready for another appointment, but I was peaceful and trusting Him.

Michael showed up soon after to take me to the appointment and I just wasn't afraid anymore. After blood was drawn they seated me in a comfortable chair that they used to administer IV Chemotherapy treatments. Well, I was trusting the Lord. I sat down and smiled at a couple next to me that were getting therapy. Michael sat in a chair on the other side of me. Then a doctor that I hadn't met before came to me. He was a retired doctor that was standing in for the young doctor that was treating me. We began talking, and he was very knowledgeable, having treated blood cancer for over thirty years. He thought I wasn't that bad. He actually asked if I had been exposed to steroids or had any infections that I knew of. He was waiting for the bone marrow results but thought whatever I had was treatable and maybe curable. Another sign of relief and words of hope. We only find peace and hope in the Lord.

Really, we had better get right with the Lord because we never know. Lo and behold, my blood test revealed that my numbers had dropped significantly, even my blood pressure and heart rate. God was settling things down.

There is hope in the Lord. We shook hands, and he said that he and or the other doctor would get back to me on Monday, after the weekend.

On the way home from the appointment, Michael took me to the grocery store for water and fruit. Another test from God came my way, out of the blue. It was very hot and the parking lot outside the grocery store was cooking. Of all times, in all of twenty-five years that we have lived here, as Michael and I were walking toward the door trying to get off the very hot pavement, a beautiful white new Cadillac, pulled up to us. I thought, "Oh, well this is it." Time to go. I wondered how I would fit my body in the car. This was better than a black hearse, right? I thought, "Well, if I have to go why not in front of the grocery store in the heat of the day." They came to pick me up in a very classy car. The window rolled down, and to my surprise, it was a very rich-looking elderly lady. The grocery store we were at was not in the type of neighborhood that you would see an expensive car, much less a wealthy lady driving it. She asked us if we could be so kind as to get her some Ensure. At first, I was surprised, but then I thought, "Well, why not?" I asked her what flavor she would like.

She looked up and said, "Strawberry." I did wonder if Michael could have been mistaken for a cart boy and maybe she thought I was a manager. She had on the real expensive dark sunglasses like my mother wears. I wasn't even sure if I could get off the hot parking lot and through the store myself, but when I saw a cane next to her, I felt sorry for her and God reminded me that I chose to live by faith and do what the Lord had for me. I put myself aside and assured her that Michael and I would pick some up for her. We did and brought it to her. She asked how much it cost, and I showed her the receipt. Then she pulled out several wallets with money and gave us a little more than what it cost us and said, "Thank you." Living by faith is great and doing those "random acts of kindness" might just be all planned by God for you. Maybe in all her money, she was in worse shape than I thought I was. It got my mind off me and on someone else and put things in perspective.

Michael dropped me off at home and then went off to the beach with his then fiancé. I went upstairs and praised God for the good report and good news. I think it will get better. The neat thing is twice when I was up there, I thought I smelled my grandmother. She had the fragrance about her like an ointment and perfume of the Lord around her. Everywhere she went, people noticed it, and it wasn't any perfume that she had put on from a store. It was the fresh aroma of the Lord. She was a very Godly and wise lady. Second Corinthians 2:15 says, "For we are unto God a sweet savor of Christ..."

God has moved upon my life. I am so thankful for everyone's prayers, especially my mother's. She said yesterday that she was quoting healing Scripture from God's Word all day, and today she was praising Him for His healing touch on my life. I knew that she would continue to seek the Lord until I was healed, off chemotherapy, and had a clean bill of health.

This morning, I felt better. I rested for once in the longest time. This past year I had so much hoped and prayed for a time-out, a time to rest. I had been so frustrated, exhausted, disgusted, worn out and beat down with the pressures of life, cost of living, demands of the job, politics and the wickedness of the world. It was consuming too much of my time and my life, stressing me out and choking out the joy of the Lord. But I didn't know how to get free and felt doomed, crushed between the pillars of commerce. I almost resigned myself to becoming a stale old government employee. I had no joy. But one last desperate prayer, and God heard my cry; I believed that when there was no way out, He had orchestrated the whole situation for my good and His glory. I was thankful for doctor's orders to rest as it provided a time to be hidden in a refuge away from pressures of life for a while. Thankful for every day: a special time to come away and be with the Lord. I do believe that God was wanting my attention for a long time, to turn away from the world, the job, all the distractions of this world and follow Him and do His work. As an answer to prayer, I believe that the Lord used this situation to break me free from bonds of that circumstance and take me to where He wants me to be and do what He wants me to do. Overall, it was the circumstance He used to answer what I had hoped for and prayed for; I am very thankful for these days of rest and the peace I feel in Him. People have questioned how this happened, the diagnosis. People have questioned the shots from the dentist to the asbestos in the building where I work. Whatever it is, I still believe that the Lord is using this experience for my good and for His glory. I have been very thankful for these days—days of seeing His hand in my life, days of waiting and resting in Him and filling me with His peace that surpasses all understanding and guards my heart and mind in Christ Jesus (John 14:27, 16:33).

Over the past days, God reminded me of His ability. In Exodus 3 and 4, God was responding to the cries of His people for deliverance and called Moses to go down to

Egypt. Moses asked the Lord how they would believe His Word. In Exodus 4:6–7, God told Moses:

> "Put now thy hand into thy bosom."
> And he put his hand in his bosom; and
> when he took it out, behold his hand was
> leprous as snow. And He said, "Put thine
> hand into thy bosom again." So he put his
> hand in his bosom and drew it out of his
> bosom, and, behold, it was turned again
> as his other flesh.

One of the lessons of that verse is that the Lord is sovereign. If he could make Moses's hand leprous, then heal it, He can do anything to assure us of His sovereignty.

My dad used to tell me that I assumed too much. I never knew what he was talking about when he would tell me that. But I do know now that we can't just assume that we can get saved, do what we want to do, not live to please the Lord, or submit to Him. We must live right and for the Lord and be mindful of His Holiness. Surrender to His Lordship is serious. We were bought with a price, and we belong to Him and must do His will for our lives. We will never be right until we find His will and do it!

In Philippians 2:12, the Word of God says that we should, "Work out our own salvation with fear and trembling."

Know that the Lord loves you. But do not take for granted what you have in Christ. Even after we get saved, we all have the potential or choice to sin again, but if we do, it will displease the Lord and it can make you ineffective, perhaps defective, even useless unless you repent before the Lord, ask Him to forgive you and turn from your wicked ways.

Scientific analysis and research information gave me some understanding and shed some light on what happened but did not answer the why question. Only God can fix something on a cellular level. Can we control or fix a problem in our genetic makeup, our weakness or wrong tendencies? I am glad for scientific research. My daughter and son-in-law are very interested and good at it. God bless the doctors in the world who seek healing. I believe that God uses drugs and alternative healing methods, but it is God who heals us. Our hope is in Him. Thankfully we, as believers, can bring whatever sickness, disease, disorder or sin under the blood of Jesus and beseech the Lord God Almighty for forgiveness and mercy and grace and deliverance and healing. I know that He has, is, and always will make everything right. He is the answer. He is the way and the truth and the life. Jesus accepted, forgave, changed, made whole and right whosoever humbly came to Him.

Determined to believe, to hold on to Him, I remembered the Word that the Lord gave me for my life and His plans for me rest assured according to Psalm 71:14–16:

> "I will hope continually" and "My mouth shall shew forth Thy righteousness and Thy salvation all the day; for I know not the numbers of" and "I will go in the strength of the Lord GOD;" and tell of His righteousness of His alone.

God is good, and His mercies are new every morning.

There is a song that I was listening to about the blood of Jesus. I thought about His blood. His blood is perfect with cleansing power. I told the Lord that I literally could not live without His blood cleansing me, my life, my blood.

I knew He heard me. I believed that He would use me and that He would do something marvelous and something glorious through this condition in His unconditional love. All I had to offer him was brokenness and strife, but He made something wonderful out of my life.

God Keeps His Promises

— ❦ —

Saturday, June 2. Brenda and Mike had just gotten home with some food, and I was hungry. The chemo made me not want to eat, but at that point I had an appetite. When I sat down at the table to eat, I remembered a time Jesus appeared to his disciples. It was the third time where He appeared to them after His resurrection. John 21 says how Jesus helped them catch many fish, and then when the disciples were done, they saw a fire on the shore. It was Jesus with fish and bread He had prepared for them. I thought of that as I was sitting there about to eat. The Lord is so tender and kind and lovingly cares for us. While I was eating and thinking about this ordeal, I knew that this would pass. The condition was just that, a condition. The Lord's love is unconditional.

After we ate, I told Brenda that I needed to write more and prepare my Sunday school lesson for the morning. I thanked her for visiting me for the day. Mike then walked her to the car, and she left to go back to Greenville. But just a few minutes after she left, she called my husband

and told him that there was a big, double full rainbow outside. Lo and behold, I looked out the window and right there in front of me was the huge full double rainbow. God reminded us that He keeps His promises. God remembers and keeps His Word. You can trust in Him with your life.

God's love is so far reaching. God is surely at work in many areas. I am amazed. The more the days go by, I see the Lord using this situation to touch many people that never would have been touched otherwise. It has become like a brilliant diamond, reflecting His work through many surfaces. The Lord opened up an avenue for Mike to reach his boss. His boss didn't quite believe him when Mike took time off to take me to the initial appointments. But after Mike explained the details of the doctor's visits and tests, suddenly his boss, a young guy, just opened up and began sharing about his life. He told Mike that he came from a very broken home and wanted to know more about his past. He had recently had a genetic test done to find out his genetic makeup. They found out that he has a blood disorder too. What the Lord is doing in my life has opened up a door for my husband to connect and reach out to this young boss and help him with doctors and treatment and hopefully share the hope of the Gospel with him.

The Little Details Matter to God

The little details matter to God. The little details make a difference. During this past March Madness, the coach of the undefeated team told the most valuable player that it was the little things that they did that made the difference. We must be sensitive to and yield to His leading, that still small voice in our spirit, and respond positively and obey Him. Yesterday morning, I felt that gentle drawing of the Lord. He was calling me to His Holy Scriptures. I almost didn't obey. There was so much work to do around the house, and I almost gave in to what I wanted to do, what I thought was important, like the Martha side. But the Lord was calling me. So many times, I foolishly put God off, eventually getting too busy doing what I think needs to be done and miss my time with Him. Have you ever had those moments? I was at a crossroad wrestling with letting go of what I wanted to do and submitting to His leading. When I got back up to my study, the Lord told me to focus on the eternal. That is something I needed to get back to as well. Put Him first! If you don't you can miss what His will is for you. God first, right? Got it! (Matt. 6:31–34, Luke 10:38–42).

One more point before I close for the evening. I glanced down at Oscar and wondered if he missed Sparkie, his best dog buddy. I looked outside the window where we buried him, my best ever puppy dog and noticed the prettiest red cardinal perched right on top of the cross we made and put on top of his grave as sweet as could be. Then I looked up and saw a firefly light up outside the window. Insignificant, small and yet meaningful. Little things do matter.

He and His Work Are Exacting

Sunday, June 3. According to Matthew 25:32–33, only God can separate the sheep from the goats. He can split hairs too. In the Old Testament, God brought plagues on the Egyptians, but not on His own people (Exodus 4–12). When He parted the Red Sea, according to Psalm 78:53, "And He led them safely, so that they did not fear; But the sea overwhelmed their enemies," not one of His people was lost or stuck in the mud. He saved every one of them and wiped out all the enemy according to Exodus 14. Only God can do mighty, powerful and infinite yet finite work. He and His work are exacting. He knows exactly what He is doing. He is intricate in His creation of snowflakes. He has a treasure full of them according to Job 38:22, yet they can melt away before they even touch the ground. He diffuses light. He is the light. He created molecules and atoms. I can trust Him on a cellular level, in my case, to take away the bad cells, like sin, in my body and keep the good ones. I am trusting Him to cleanse my blood and make it right and in right order. And you can trust Him too for whatever. Do you follow me? Whatever you need or whatever you are desperate for, because He loves you, Philippians 4:19 says, "He shall supply all your need according to His riches in glory by Christ Jesus."

I will share as many truths as I felt led to write down, my testimony, that I am living proof of the power of God that saves lives in hopes that it will encourage you and help to build your faith in Him. It is our faith in Him that saves us.

The battles we wage are spiritual in nature. Second Corinthians 10:4–5b says, "For the weapons of our warfare are not carnal, but mighty in God for pulling down strongholds; casting down imaginations and every high thing that exalteth itself against the knowledge of God."

In John 10:10, Jesus said, "The thief cometh not, but for to steal, and to kill, and to destroy; I have come that they may have life, and that they may have it more abundantly."

The theme of our adult Sunday school classes happens to be the abundant life. Life is good, and abundant life is from God.

According to 1 John 5:4, "For whatever is born of God overcometh the world: and this is the victory that has overcometh the world, even our faith."

We go from glory to glory and victory to victory.

Early that morning, I went to get matches. Every Sunday morning, I light three candles, one for the Father, one for Jesus and one for the Holy Spirit. It is a little hard to reach the candles because they are positioned in ascending order between two panes of glass that are fit narrowly together. But when the candles are lit, the light illuminates Our Father's Prayer, which is inscribed on the front pane of glass. A lady who used to attend our adult Sunday school gave it to me. It is very special to me.

When I opened the box of matches to light the candles, there was just one match left to light the three candles. I thought about how I was going to light the three candles with one match. I needed more matches, but it was the only one left in the box. Then a thought crossed my mind. What if that one match represented the amount of days of life I had left? What if we only had three strikes in life? That was my dad's motto, "Three strikes and you're out." I had only one strike with this. Well, I got the match ready to strike the flint and thought, "I had better not blow it. I have only one chance to get all three candles lit." But when I went to strike the match on the flint, the head completely broke off the stick. Drats, that's it, what now? I quickly went to the kitchen hoping to find more matches, more time. When I opened the cabinet door and looked next to a bottle of oil, thankfully I saw a whole pack and another box. I was relieved. I felt as if it was a sign that the Lord was going to give me more days to display, lift up, illuminate or let His Light, Him and His Word shine through me. Matthew 5:14–16 says,

> "Ye are the light of the world. A city that is set on a hill cannot be hid. Neither do they light a candle and put it under a bushel, but on a candlestick; and it giveth light unto all that are in the house. Let your light so shine before men, that they may see your good works and glorify your Father in heaven."

Remember the song, "This Little Light of Mine" by Harry Dixon Loes? Are you going to let your light shine? Don't hide it under a bushel and don't let Satan blow it out. Let it shine, shine, shine. Let the Light, Jesus, shine through you and give our Father in heaven the glory. Our days are really numbered by the Lord and every day is a privilege to be used of Him and serve Him and do His will.

One more thing happened that had a message worth sharing. I had to check the calendar on my kitchen wall, but the nail that was holding the calendar on the wall along with several papers fell out. Everything fell down. As I picked up all the papers and the calendar and nailed it back on the wall, I noticed that the calendar was from Master's

Real Estate. A friend from church owns that business, and she sends me a calendar every year. It was another reminder that He owns our property, our time, and He places us on His calendar according to His plan for our life. The predestined appointments have been prearranged for our life by God.

Pay Attention

⸏⸏⸏⸏⸏ ℘ ⸏⸏⸏⸏⸏

Monday, June 4. This morning my alarm went off, and right away the Lord urged me to get up and pay attention. The preacher's voice on the radio that morning was different. It was remarkably authoritative and voluminous. I grabbed my robe, ran to the kitchen to get a pad of paper and a pen, jumped back up on my bed and started taking notes just as fast as I could write.

The message was from the book of Joshua 5:13–Joshua 6. At that point, the message was so good that if it was the last one my ears heard, it made life worth living and the message worth sharing. Before the message came on, I had thought about many greats of the faith that had endured fiery trials and tests of faith. Many had battled cancer and come through to victory. When I tuned back into the message, the pastor explained that when God has a great work to do, it would be the person of faith that would so called, get the contract. That resonated with my soul.

So the diagnosis became more of a contract of faith. It became more than a human battle and a challenge. It became part of the good fight of faith. It was a trial of faith. Proverbs 17:3 says, "The refining pot is for silver and the furnace for gold; but the Lord trieth the hearts."

The tool God was using to try my heart was a face-to-face life-threatening situation that came from within. What is God using in your life? We all have our outer battles. Even as much as I exercised and tried to eat right, I couldn't save myself. My salvation and healing, as well as yours, will not be on our own work but totally dependent on the grace of God.

There were a few more points about the story that are very applicable, helpful and timeless as it is drawn from God's Word. So the challenge was before Joshua. The walls of Jericho were between him and God's promise. Joshua was a conqueror, captain, and a problem solver. But the Lord, strong and mighty was ahead of him. Do you see the Lord ahead of you, leading you into battle into victory in order to give Him the glory? The Lord appeared to him before he could ever even figure out the how-to; how would he get over the "bigger than life" high walls surrounding the city that housed the enemy camp?

Joshua 5:13 says, "He lifted up his eyes and looked, and behold, there stood a man over against him with His sword drawn in His hand."

According to Joshua 5:13–15 it was the Commander of the Army of the LORD of Hosts, the preincarnate Savior

Jesus (not God the Father because He cannot be seen by human mortal flesh other than Jesus, [see John 6:46]) that appeared to Joshua to give him *His plan* to victory. God was going to work it out. They were not going to have to go over the walls, or under the walls or have to use canons, dynamite or even a Trojan horse to bulldoze their way in. God will do whatever it takes for us too. Isaiah 55:9 says, "For as the heavens are higher than the Earth, so are My Ways higher than your ways, and My thoughts than your thoughts."

Second Samuel 22:31 says, "As for God, His way is perfect."

Isaiah 43:16 says, "Thus saith the LORD, which maketh a way in the sea, and a path in the mighty waters."

And in John 14:6 Jesus says, "I am the way."

Joshua was literally going to walk by faith. The next seven plus days, He was going to live by faith, whether it made sense or not. It required complete trust and unquestioning allegiance to God. No second guessing and no swerving or deviation and no divided heart. Apart from God, the pressure would have been too immense as the whole nation of Israel was counting on his leadership. All eyes were on Joshua and he had better have heard from God. There are many lessons in this story about doing and living God's way and quietly waiting on Him for what seemed an impossible situation, like needing a way to make the walls come down. Joshua never questioned God. Joshua just followed the Lord's orders. He didn't whine or complain or try to figure it out on his own. He just followed the instructions that the Lord gave him. He was a good and Godly leader.

Joshua logistically organized the men of valor, the armed men, then the seven priests with the trumpets of rams' horns, the Ark of the Lord, the rear guard and the Israelites. They walked around the city once a day for six days. On the seventh day, after they all walked around the wall seven times, the priests blew their trumpets, all God's people shouted with a loud shout and God miraculously made the walls of Jericho shake and crumble before their very eyes. Then according to Joshua 6:5b, "And the people shall ascend up every man straight before him."

God just laid it all out for them and led them to victory. They only needed to obey God's Word and walk by faith, pursue and possess what the Lord promised them.

We need to train ourselves to take our eyes off the "bigger than life," seemingly unsurmountable problems and focus on the Lord Jesus who always leads us to victory. It doesn't matter what the numbers say, God is greater than any obstacle that comes between us and His promise. Remember, according to Hebrews 11:1: "Faith is the substance of things hoped for, and the evidence of things not seen."

Joshua's faith was exhibited when he and God's people went forward by faith to claim what God had already given them. They did exactly as the Lord had commanded Joshua and walked toward the victory. By faith the walls of Jericho came tumbling down. When His people, the whole congregation, went forward by faith in obedience and claimed their possession, God gave them the victory. God moved and made the thick and impenetrable walls fall. There was no way without the Lord. He made what was impossible with man, even an army of men, possible.

Yesterday the Lord allowed me to teach my Sunday school class. It is a five-year-old class which the Lord has blessed me with every Sunday for the past twenty years. I consider all the children and my co-worker extra special treasures and blessings from the Lord. The way I see it is that I get a touch from heaven every Sunday. Matthew 18:10b says, "Of these little ones; for I say to you, that in heaven their angels always behold the face of My Father which is in heaven."

In addition, my co-worker can run circles around me, does the administrative work, keeps me informed, and knows how to settle them down. I have learned so much from her, and I couldn't do a Sunday without her. She has stayed humble by staying with me all these years.

One of the points of the lesson was to not focus on what the devil tries to bring on us but to magnify and look to what the Lord is doing. The Lord is bigger than any wall or obstacle that comes between us and His promise. Remember, Joshua still had to work out his faith, right? The Lord showed him exactly how to and what to do to overcome and get the victory.

We need to live by faith whether or not it makes sense. God wants unquestioned obedience from us.

Good thing is that faith is merely agreeing with God's Word, what He already has spoken. He spoke absolute truth in the universe before we even had faith to respond to His Word. Our faith is speaking what God has already said.

If we can trust the Lord for our salvation, then we can trust in Him for anything and everything. His blood cleanses us from all unrighteousness.

Remember to trust and obey is to be happy.

Whatever you are facing, He is your hope; He is your enablement; He is the answer.

His Mercies Are New Every Morning

Tuesday, June 5. His mercies are new every morning, according to Lamentations 3:22–23. God and His love is so much. He pours out His Spirit and reveals truth. John 9:32 says, "Since the world began was it not heard that any man opened the eyes of one that was born blind."

He still opens our eyes to behold Him. He is good. Turn to Him. Proverbs 1:23 says, "Turn you at My reproof: behold, I will pour out my spirit unto you, I will make known My words unto you."

God is faithful and able to perform that which He promised, according to Romans 4:21, "And being fully persuaded that, He promised, He was able also to perform."

And Hebrews 10:23, "Let us hold fast the profession of our faith without wavering; (for He is faithful that promised)."

Last night before I could finish writing some things the Lord showed me earlier that morning, God impressed on me another verse regarding how important it is to meditate day and night. Then my way, and your way, will be prosperous. Joshua 1:7–9 says,

> Only be thou strong and very courageous, that thou mayest observe to do according to all the law, which Moses my servant commanded thee; turn not from it to the right hand or to the left, that thou mayest prosper whithersoever thou goest. This Book of the Law shall not depart out of thy mouth, but thou shall meditate therein day and night, that thou mayest observe to do according to all that is written therein: For then thou will make your way prosperous, and then thou shalt have good success. Have I not commanded thee? Be strong and of a good courage; be not afraid, neither be dismayed: for the LORD your God is with you whithersoever thou goest.

Earlier in the day I came across a picture of a field of yellow flowers. Yellow flowers always remind of my grandmother who was a prayer warrior, prayed for my salvation, and is now at home with the Lord. The picture made me think of heaven, fields of yellow flowers, sunny, spacious blue skies and peacefulness. Later I saw a sketch of a globe with the words, do great things, which inspired and encouraged me to do great things and to the left of it is a picture of a globe. Going forward, that was inspiring and an encouragement to do great things in the world for the Lord.

We Have a Very Bright Future

─── ❧ ───

Thursday, June 7. Again, as with every day, His mercies are new every morning, indeed! Whatever; I mean whatever may come, I will, we will, according to Psalm 92:2, "Declare Your lovingkindness in the morning and Your faithfulness every night."

Again, God reminded me of another verse in His Word that gave me hope for living. Hebrews 4:12 says, "For the word of God is quick, and powerful, and sharper than any two-edged sword, piercing even to the dividing asunder of soul and spirit, and of bone and marrow, and is a discerner of thoughts and intents of the heart."

Surely, His Word can pierce right down to where no man can, and wield His eternal sharp and powerful Sword to do His work.

The entrance of His Word gives light and life. If we have Jesus in our hearts and have repented of our sin and confessed our sins, His blood covers us and redeems our life for eternity. We have a very bright future. His Word in our hearts gives us light and life and in Him is no darkness at all. Whatever darkness, evil or sin tries to overtake our life, it will not prosper because of God's Word in our life. According to Isaiah 54:17, "No weapon formed against you shall prosper."

He overcomes the dark. Also remember John 10:10 where Jesus told us, "The thief cometh not but for to steal, and to kill, and to destroy. I am come that they may have life and have it more abundantly."

I mentioned this earlier, but I say again, if we turn to the Lord, we will be built up. Job 22:23 says, "If thou return to the Almighty, thou shalt be built up."

After I had reviewed my notes I had written on a pad of paper, I realized that the top of the pad given to me by my faithful friend at church says, "Faith plants seed. Love makes it grow."

So far, I surely hope and pray that I have been a blessing to you. Remember that His blood was shed for you and His body was broken for you. I believe I was broken to get right and to share all these things with you. So I consider this a treasured trial or trial filled with treasures.

Everyone wants more time; even my doctor told me he was buying more time until he figured out what to do with me. Jesus bought us. He essentially owns our time, the days of life. He is the one who can extend our life and give us time to do what He wants us to do.

Do you know that we are time limited special editions for the Lord and only God Himself determines the days of our lives? He is our Alpha and Omega. He is the beginning of life and the ending of life.

This past week has changed my life forever. It has been my passion week. It has brought me to the point of realizing I need to lay my life down. It is merely corruptible and worthless without Him living through me. My life, your life, the flesh with its passions need to be crucified if we want to go on as a useful and effective Christian and obey completely. The only way to do God's will daily, is to crucify the flesh with its passions and desires. I am praying for His mercy and grace and enablement for me and you to do this and to live through His resurrection power.

Jesus took away all my sins, washed me clean, and He can do the same for you. I believe He heard me, and I receive His answer and healing. I heard Him in my spirit tell me to go and sin no more. Surely, He saves us to serve others. We are to get up, roll up our mats and go on to what the Lord has for us. Carry the Light, shine for Him and share the gospel that Jesus saves.

Can't You See?

In the meantime, all the doctors need to see are the numbers. Their measuring stick is test results. Some believers needed to see Jesus's nail-pierced hands and feet. They won't believe until they see but we need to believe and then see. Remember what Jesus said in John 20:29, "Jesus saith unto him, Thomas, because thou hast seen me, thou has believed: blessed are they that have not seen, and yet have believed."

No matter what the count, the Lord told me that He would take care of the numbers. If you were to count, keep the numbers of how many times you have sinned, let the Lord down, the numbers would be staggering. But He has forgiven everyone who has pleaded the blood of Jesus. Believe Him, receive it forgiveness, healing, restoration, just as when you trusted Him for your salvation. He makes all things new.

The joy of the Lord is my strength, your strength. This present affliction is all for the glory of the Lord to be revealed through my life. Second Corinthians 4:17 says, "For our light affliction, which is but for a moment, worketh for us a far more exceeding and eternal weight of glory;"

I prayed that the Lord would go down to my very core, where only He could touch, my bone marrow and take this so called disease from me and fix the broken chromosomes. I do know that when we are weak, He is strong. Second Corinthians 12:9 says, "And he said unto me, My grace is sufficient for thee: for my strength is made perfect in weakness. Most gladly therefore will I rather glory in my infirmities, that the power of Christ may rest upon me"

I was remembering when Jesus healed lepers. In Luke 17:11–17, Jesus had mercy on the lepers who cried out to Him. He cleansed lepers from the deteriorating disease and restored life. I believe that He granted it: healing, mercy, and restoration. He has given me a peace that passes my understanding and guards my heart. I pray that the doctor's office will respond well. Someday our work and trials will be over. And you and I will come in and go out with rejoicing as we trust in Him.

Love Our Enemies

Since I still have a listening ear, I would like to share some more truths that the Lord showed me. I hope that it will help you as well. It is one more area that I had to get right in. It goes down to a bedrock issue that I had often wondered about. It is about praying for our enemies and them that have spitefully used us. It is a daily battle. They take their own problems and twist them and put them on us as if we have the problem. They fabricate untruths to justify their mistakes and problems, make mountains out of mole hills, treat us unfairly, take our good ideas, implement them and take the credit. It is most unbearable. It is unspoken persecution and spiritual warfare. This continuing battle also has to do with the constant twisting, distortion, perversion, cover up and avoidance of the truth which is from Satan, the father of lies and perverter of truth. The devil is a master at this and that is how anyone of his followers operates. Many a time in the gospels, the Pharisees tried to twist the truth of Jesus. According to John 15:20, if they hate Jesus, they will hate me and you, because we are followers of Jesus.

This is very hard. They would undermine our very sanity if they could. I prayed that the Lord would take them or us away, destroy our enemies or take them out of the office. I didn't even care about the eternal destiny of their souls anymore. They vexed my soul, and I became distraught with them, wrote them off, wished evil and death on them. It still makes me cry. They tried to undo me. Have you ever been put over a barrel or had someone twist your arm or put you in a head lock? It isn't nice. But I remembered that Jesus prayed for the ones who mocked Him and persecuted Him and nailed His body to the cross. That is what some ungodly people want to do to us. But in His strength alone, I endured remembering Hebrews 12:2–3, which says,

> Who for the joy that was set before Him endured the cross, despising the shame, and is set down at the right hand of the throne of God. For consider Him who endured such contradiction from sinners against Himself, lest ye become weary and faint in your minds.

Second Corinthians 4:8–9 says, "We are troubled on every side, yet not distressed; we are perplexed, but not in despair; persecuted, but not forsaken; cast down but not destroyed."

Also, being mindful of Ephesians 6:11–13, which says,

> Put on the whole armor of God, that
> ye may be able to stand against the wiles
> of the devil. For we do not wrestle against
> flesh and blood, but against principalities,
> against powers, against the rulers of the
> darkness of this age, against spiritual hosts
> of wickedness in the heavenly places.
> Wherefore, take up the whole armor of
> God, that ye may be able to withstand in
> the evil day, and having done all, to stand.

I remembered the story of Jonah and started back-peddling fast and repented of my attitude toward them that were persecuting me. I tried to resolve within myself to go and be the godly witness He might want me to be to them. Jonah came to the end of himself in the fish. It was the tool of correction that God used in his life, the place and time to repent. Whatever situation, diagnosis, hardship God uses, I encourage you to understand that and change, get right, and be thankful that God is willing to use you. Submit to His calling and mission and to His mercy and grace.

Later my husband directed me to Luke 10:25–37. In the parable that Jesus told us, the lawyer who was testing Jesus asked Jesus how to inherit eternal life. Jesus asked him what the law said, so the lawyer quoted the Old Testament scripture in verse 27, "Thou shalt love the LORD thy God with all thy heart, with all thy soul, with all thy strength, and with all thy mind, and thy neighbor as thyself."

When the lawyer further tested Jesus by asking Him who his neighbor is, Jesus told him of the parable of the good Samaritan. Basically, our neighbor is anyone in need. Even people in the office. They might be the way they are because they have never been shown compassion or the love of God.

So we are to love our enemies and "pray for them that spitefully use" us according to Luke 6:28. But it is only possible to do that with the love of God.

God extinguished the thought that my enemies should burn because of their wickedness. Sometimes in the Old Testament, in the Psalms, death was wished on the enemies of God's people. A lot of times God helped His people fight and then led them to victory. That is what caused me to waiver in my prayers toward them and justify my anger and thoughts toward them. But as I was flipping through scripture I came across Ezekiel 33:11, which says, "Say unto them; As I live', saith the Lord GOD, 'I have no pleasure in the death of the wicked, but that the wicked turn from his way and live: turn ye, turn ye from your evil ways; for why should ye die, O house of Israel?"

God sent Elijah to King Ahab to get him to stop leading His people to worship idols (read 1 Kings 16–17) and God sent Jonah to Nineveh to give them another chance to repent and turn from their wicked ways and serve the Lord. So after thinking about these and other examples it gave me peace and assurance that in the Old and New Testament God wills to save and He wills that people will turn from their sin. Also, a friend reminded me that He saved me even though I did not deserve His love, salvation and grace in my life.

So I withstood the battles and determined to forgive and love them through it all.

After a while God changed my heart and gave me a Godly unconditional love for them.

Realizing how sinful I had been, I asked the Lord to forgive me for that evil and I promised that I would not wish death on the wicked anymore. Rather my prayer will be that they turn from their wicked ways as I have so that we all may live. You and I need to endure and continue to pray for them that vex our souls and trust the Lord with the outcome. As Christians, as Godly witnesses, we are to love our enemies, not curse them. Remember the old song that goes, "They will know we are Christians by our love, by our love, yes they will know we are Christians by our love."

Our Only Hope

Friday, June 8. Couldn't have agreed more with a statement I heard early that morning which was that the only hope for the moral deterioration of our nation is repentance before God. The blood of Jesus can wash away our sin, restore us and make it as if we never sinned. Years ago, my daughter had a friend who occasionally wore a t-shirt that had a saying on it, "The beatings will continue until the morals are restored." I never forgot that, and often as I looked around in the world thought how true that saying was and is now. Order and peace happen when we get right with God. Have you ever heard anyone say that they thought genetic deformities were due to "the fall?" Our fallen condition leaves us all in a broken state. I do understand and believe when we fall into sin, it can trigger a deformity in our Godly character. If that is true, our only hope again is repentance and getting right before God.

There is something else I feel that I need to share and impress upon you out of this ordeal. Do not shrug off or even tolerate little sin. Address them before they wreak havoc. Keep short accounts with God. We need to pray for His grace to help us have the determination and resolve to stand fast as Christians, resist the devil, keep ourselves yielded, and under the control of the Holy Spirit, and in alignment with His Holy Scriptures.

Pardon and a Real-Life Sentence

lso, there was a story on the evening news that so moved me that I have to share this too. A man did something bad and was put into jail, served time, changed his life, got out and was doing just fine. But then some weird, out-of-the-blue lawyer judged him still guilty, and he was put back into jail. None of the details were disclosed but he needs prayer and a pardon. Just like anyone else, thinking life is good and then out of the blue, something hits hard, unexpected bad news, like a report that threatens our life and we need to cry out to God for a pardon, wipe our slate clean and trust God for an eternal life sentence.

God also showed me that our day-to-day and even moment-to-moment choices matter. We have an influence and make an impact on the world we live in and will leave a legacy for future generations. We need to be mindful of our holy potential throughout our hectic schedules and daily living. We all have an eternal purpose and should not lose sight of that during the hours of our lives. We also need to look past and through the times of conflict and challenges, look for the Lord, and believe in Him for the miracles to impact the people we influence and paths we cross everywhere.

The Cancer of Sin

G od had put First Corinthians 5 on my mind. This spoke to my heart as well. Paul addresses the church regarding immorality that defiled the body of Christ. First Corinthians 5:6–8 says,

> Your glorying is not good. Knoweth ye not that a little leaven leavens the whole lump? Purge out the old leaven, that ye may be a new lump, as ye are unleaven… neither with the leaven of malice and wickedness; but with the unleavened bread of sincerity and truth.

I know that there are other references of where Jesus talked about leavened bread but that is not the Scripture He drew to my attention now. There is another point He was bringing to my attention specific to the situation at hand. The leaven is malice and wickedness. Noah Webster's 1828 Edition of *American Dictionary of The English Language* defines *malice*, in the noun form, as "extreme enmity of heart, malevolence; a disposition to injure others without cause, from the personal gratification or from a spirit of revenge; unprovoked malignity or spite" or as a verb, "to regard with extreme ill will."

Furthermore, *wickedness* is defined as "departure from the rules of the divine law; evil disposition or practices; immorality; crime; sin; sinfulness; corrupt manners."

Heard enough. Doesn't need too much more explanation. I felt convicted. Another area that I needed to repent of down in my heart, the part that is between me and the Lord, and rather walk in sincerity and truth. According to 2 Timothy 2:17, ungodliness and its message can spread like cancer. If you have a bad cell, it can eventually spread and become cancer. The doctor said that leukemia is just a word used for a blood disorder. Something is not right. Christians can have a disorder or a dysfunction spiritually.

The blood that flows through our veins needs to be right. We don't want it to be corrupted and dysfunctional. Thankfully, when we ask Jesus into our hearts and lives we have the God gene in us. Take heed fellow believer not to live in a way that makes us defective to the One we should be loyal to and pledge our allegiance to. Don't do anything that could cause corruption or offense to His blood and His work in our lives. His blood is perfect, and cleanses our imperfections and sin-tainted blood. We were bought with a price and need to honor Him always. The marrow is deeper than the gut of a human; it is where the red blood cells, platelets and white blood cells are made which then circulate throughout the entire body. I asked the Lord if He would forgive me if I had acted with malice or wickedness. Leprosy always coincided with sin. And Jesus healed the lepers and made them whole. That is what I hope: the Lord will bring order to the disorder in my blood, through His perfect blood that forgives me from sin.

This morning my son's strong-willed stubborn little Shih Tzu, named Oscar, brought another challenge or opportunity to my life. I turned my back for a minute while I was tending to my son's Great Dane/Labrador named Flapjack. But just at a turn-around point, Oscar snuck off into the woods through the poison ivy. By the time I looked up, he was well off down the trail through the woods. Because of the poison ivy and poison oak, once he has gone down in there, I could not go in and get him out because I am very allergic to both. I called him and whistled until Flap and I gave up. Helpless again, I started praying that the Lord would bring him out. I waited another minute but no Oscar. I turned to go back home and left it in the Lord's hands. But about fifty feet down the road, Oscar came running up behind us, and with such delight, he ran right past us. I was glad that the Lord brought him out of the woods and into the clear. Let Him bring you out of the woods and the entangling poison ivy. When we really have exhausted ourselves on situations that we have no control over and put them in the Lord's hands, and go on walking in faith, trusting that He will take care of the matter, He always comes through for us. Glory to His name again!

We do go on from Glory to Glory. Every situation can be used by God to bring Glory to Himself.

The Pruning

❦

Pruning. The following is a Wikipedia definition of pruning (Wikipedia contributors, "Pruning," Wikipedia, the Free Encyclopedia,

https://en.wikipedia.org/w/index.php?title=Pruning&oldid=964578691(accessedOctober10,2018):

> Pruning is a horticultural and silvicultural practice involving the selective removal of certain parts of a plant, such as branches, buds, or roots. Reasons to prune plants include deadwood removal, shaping (by controlling or redirecting growth), improving or sustaining health, reducing risk from falling branches, preparing nursery specimens for transplanting, and both harvesting and increasing the yield or quality of flowers and fruits.

The practice entails *targeted* removal of diseased, damaged, dead, non-productive, structurally unsound, or otherwise unwanted tissue from crop and landscape plants. In general, the smaller the branch that is cut, the easier it is for a woody plant to compartmentalize the wound and thus…

Limit the potential for pathogen intrusion and decay.

Have you ever watched the procedure done? Gardeners or landscapers use shears or saws or maybe other tools to cut and reshape. Some of the cuts seem brutal and extensive. After the deep cuts on the trees are made and all that is left is bare, I am always amazed that anything grows back. It is like the Lord has used this condition to prune me, my life. I believe God's work is all inclusive. Similar to the way a gardener prunes, cuts off the bad, removes the dead branches to improve the rest of the health of a tree or bush, I believe that the Lord is pruning my life and reshaping, remolding, controlling direction or causing redirection in my life. It has taken me down to my knees. The good thing is that as time goes on, He also brings new growth, healing, and restoration. He brings new life because He prunes the right way and in the right seasons. God's pruning process in our lives can cause new branches, like areas of ministry, that sprout out in more places than before the pruning, and the trees end up shaped better and grow higher and farther. Remember according to John 15:1–5, Jesus is the vine and we are the branches. Let's stay yielded to Jesus and our Father as The vinedresser.

A little over two weeks ago, I had no clue of what was to come. After I hung up the shocking phone call, the scariest thought came to my mind, "prepare for a funeral." The thought seemed to come out of nowhere. I didn't know if it was from God or a bad thought from the devil. Chills went down my spine. I really didn't know what to do next. After the doctor's report was confirmed, I did start planning for the end of my life.

As the next few days went by, so many prayers of people were storming heaven for my life. James 5:16 says, "Confess your faults one to another, that ye may be healed. The effectual fervent prayers of a righteous man availeth much."

Everyone's prayers were my lifeline, and God's Word was my hope.

Mike told me something that made sense this morning. Before he headed out to work, I shared something that had happened earlier that morning and then he asked me if I remembered how the Lord told me about preparing for a funeral. He went on to say that he thought that the

Lord meant a funeral for me, myself, my life and to put it to death, the plans I made for the rest of my life. Just as new leaves and branches sprout after a pruning, our new life in Him will start growing in ways we never could have imagined. Not my ways, not your ways, but His ways. As Christians, we are to die to self and live for God. Galatians 2:20 says, "I am crucified with Christ; nevertheless I live: yet not I, but Christ liveth in me: and the life which I now live in the flesh I live by faith in the Son of God, who loved me and gave Himself for me."

I heard him and really came to terms with that truth. So after I accepted that into my life I thought, "It is done," got it. Now the life I live is in Him and what I live for is for Him, His story. Matthew 16:25 says, "For whosoever will save his life will lose it, but whoever loses his life for My sake shall find it."

Upcoming Days

— ❧ —

S aturday, June 9. Today is my birthday. My aunt sent me a verse, 3 John 2 which says, "Beloved, I wish above all things that thou mayest prosper and be in health, just as thy soul prospereth."

It was the Scripture she wrote down in my birthday card. I took that to heart. How thankful I am to start another year of my life in Christ today! I am very thankful for everyone who has been praying for me and pray that the Lord will bless you for reaching out to me and bringing my life before the Lord. I was thankful to spend the day cleaning the house and the dogs, tidying up, responding to phone calls, praying and praising Him for all the days He has given me, thankful for everything He has done and all the answers to prayers. I enjoyed an early dinner and cake with my Mike, Brenda, Henry, Heather, Michael, and Joshua and felt overwhelmed with love and support. What is to come in the upcoming days are in His hands. Surely, goodness and mercy shall follow me all the days of my life. Continue to hope in Him and cheerfully wait on Him. I am excited, anticipating great things from Him this year. Every day from here on out is a day I will walk by faith.

Sunday, June 10. Early in the morning my mother was on my mind. As I prayed for her, the Lord put it on my heart to tell her not to worry. He said, "Behold, I have overcome." John 16:33 says, "Be of good cheer; 'I have overcome the world.'" He knew that my mother was worried and distraught, understandably so, but He did not want her to fret one more minute because He has overcome. He is our peace, and she needed to be reminded and we need to be reminded and encouraged that the Lord has overcome disease, as well as sin and death.

The Lord reminded me of Jeremiah 33:3, which says, "Call unto Me, and I will answer thee, and show thee great and mighty things which thou knowest not."

Almost daily I look in the mirror and quote Psalms 103:1–5, which says,

> Bless the Lord, O my soul; and all that
> is within me, bless His holy name! Bless
> the LORD, O my soul, and forget not all
> His benefits: Who forgiveth all thine iniq-
> uities; Who healeth all thy diseases; Who
> redeemeth thy life from destruction; Who
> crowneth thee with lovingkindness and

tender mercies; Who satisfieth thy mouth
with good things; so that thy youth is
renewed like the eagle's.

From time to time, I had wondered about the individual
verses, the order of them, and how they are all-inclusive. This
morning the Lord showed me that first He forgives, then He
heals, and then He redeems our life. Also, He crowns us with
His lovingkindness and His tender mercies. He satisfies us,
not just feeds us, but satisfies our mouth with good things,
so that our youth is renewed just like the eagle's strength is
renewed. The rest of the chapter has more of His promises
to us, but these first five verses reveal a process and order in
the way the Lord works. He is such a good care giver of our
lives. Now these verses are much more applicable to me, and
I understand His move upon my life better. It is all a process
of transformation for us to be more like Him.

Stories have been told about how an eagle goes through
a molting process at around age forty. It involves a retreat
to its nest very high up to a mountain top where it knocks
off its beak, its talons, and plucks out all its old worn out
feathers. Why, you may ask? It is to regrow a new beak, new
talons and new feathers. The process is estimated to take
150 days. Then the eagle's strength is renewed, and it can
go on to live another thirty years. Isaiah 40:31 says, "But

they that wait upon the LORD shall renew their strength; they shall mount up with wings like eagles, they shall run and not be weary, they shall walk and not faint."

Most of the past week I have been up in my study. It is nowhere near the top of a mountain, but the view is always one of my favorites. Outside the two windows is a view overlooking many trees, the athletic fields of my church, the woods behind it, and part of the neighborhood. This is my retreat. It is where I break down before the Lord, cry out to God, pray, praise God, and where I have been seeking the Lord during this ordeal in my life.

Trying to get through the tearing down process of the chemotherapy, which is meant to purge the body of all dead cells and retard cancerous growth, is rigorous. I believe that the Lord either allows, arranges, or appoints situations, for our good and for His glory. I have to believe that this situation has been orchestrated by Him and is a tool from Him. His work in progress. While you and I are under God's construction, being transformed into His image, be sure to keep a thankful heart and attitude and "wait patiently," according to James 5:7–11.

We are all soldiers of the cross according to 2 Timothy 2:3: "Thou therefore endure hardness, as a good soldier of Jesus Christ."

The LORD of hosts, Jesus Christ, is our captain. We don't tell him what to do. He graciously gives us assignments. Job didn't ask for all his suffering, but after he forgave his friend, God restored everything. We learned from what the Lord did in Job's life, and I hope that God uses what is going on in your life to draw you and others closer to Him. Be careful to give Him the Glory for His work through you.

This morning, we didn't make it to church because our air conditioning unit broke. We had to wait for a repair man to come to the house. It was getting warm in the house. Just around the time our church service started, my husband's friend showed up and fixed our unit, and it brought us much needed relief. But again, it made me think of all the lives whose souls and lives are hanging in the eternal balance teetering on the edge of where they will spend eternity. Have I done what I could so far with my time to rescue the perishing by telling them the good news that if they choose to believe, Jesus can forgive their sin and save them from the never ending, eternal flames of hell? We all need to ask ourselves that question. The heat of the summer always reminds me of the relentless fires in hell and people that will spend eternity there just because we didn't tell them about Jesus or because they chose Him not.

This morning I saw a picture of a very mountainous area. No level ground at all. The mountains were rugged and sharp looking. I saw a man and a woman climbing up one side. The man got to a plateau and was helping the woman up. The view of seemingly endless mountains seemed overwhelming, and I wondered how they even got to where they were. I could just imagine them reaching the top. Then I noticed how sharp the old rocks seemed, even appearing abrasive. Maybe the Lord is using this abrasive condition to grind, polish, and clean my hard surface. The abrasiveness of this situation surely is helping me get a grip on Him and His Word to pull myself up.

The Candle

This morning, I noticed the candle that Heather, Michael's fiancé, lit the evening before my birthday, was still burning. Near noon time it was still burning. The other day I had checked the candle and thought it was near the end. Actually, I was surprised Heather got it lit. The fact that it burned all night into today and this evening now was a wonder to me. I was glad the light was still on. Around noon time, I pointed it out to my husband, and he said, "Laverne." I asked him what that had to do with the candle. Nowhere on the label was the word or name Laverne. He asked me if I remembered Laverne from work. Laverne is a prayer warrior where he works. I think she gave me the candle a year ago when Brenda got engaged or when my favorite puppy dog died. She really has a ministry and is very sensitive to the Lord's leading. She didn't even know me but gave me that candle and a beautiful Thomas Kinkaid planning calendar. Just the fact that the candle came from a very Godly prayer intercessor and that it just keeps burning, encouraged me to keep oil in my lamp and keep burning for Him.

That Thou Mayest Prosper

Monday, June 11. The word of the day came to me early this morning. It was in a text from my aunt, but I knew it was from the Lord. It was 3 John 2: "Beloved, I wish above all things that thou mayest prosper and be in health, even as your soul prospereth." It was the same verse she gave me for my birthday.

My appointment was in the afternoon so while my husband took my oldest son to the ortho appointment for his knee, I continued to pray hard. I had never anointed my home and everything in it with oil and prayed the consecration prayer over my house. I believe in it. I went all over the house, touched every door post, prayed that His blood would cover it and anoint whoever comes in and goes out, minister and bless them. I prayed over the frames of the windows so that whoever looks out would in some way see the Lord. In Exodus, God had Moses brush the door posts with the blood of a lamb so that the angel of death would pass over. I prayed in the name of the Father, Son and Holy Ghost, and made the sign of the cross like the Catholics do and asked the Lord to forgive all sin in every room, break the power of anything evil and displeasing in our home from the past eighteen years and consecrated our home to God and declared it a house of prayer and ministry. Amen.

At the appointed time, I drove myself to my appointment. I was happy and at peace and felt good. The usual blood work was drawn. While they took the sample to the lab, the nurse checked my vitals, and for the first time in years, my blood pressure hit the mark. I think all the rest recently was much needed for my body. Everything, all the problems that had been stressing me out had to go and my body had to settle down. I hadn't felt this good since years ago. The Lord was renewing my strength.

About ten more minutes passed, and the nurse came around the corner with the papers and said, "I have fantastic news," and told me that my numbers looked great. She showed me that all the bad numbers had dropped significantly, and the good numbers were holding.

This is the report of the Lord!

If I did not share the following I would not be sharing everything that the Lord did as a result of everyone's prayers for me and my family. Some of you will have to bear with me; others will see the move of the Lord and continue to praise Him for such far-reaching, all-inclusive work. Around dinner time my other son, Michael, came home to take the dogs out. They are his dogs, but since his place does not have any space, we are keeping them until he and his fiancé get married in November and find a place with a good-sized yard in a good location for them both. When he came in the house he said, "Mom, why is there oil all over the garage door handle?" At first, I shrugged my shoulders and said that I did not know, that I had not touched the door handle with anything. Then I remembered, earlier that day, I had felt led to pray over the garage. I was reluctant because I didn't think God could do anything with our garage as it is a huge mess. But I went outside anyway and gently touched the three posts of the garage with oil and prayed God's blessing and use of it. Then I went inside, tried to overlook the mess of tools, car parts, bicycles, papers, books, sports, gardening, hunting and camping equipment and other miscellaneous things that Mike had gathered over the years and prayed that the Lord would even use that space. It is Mike's garage. Any woman would be like "heavens, whatever." It is a real man's cave for sure. Then it hit me. That oil on the door is the anointing from the Lord for Mike's ministry. We have been praying about a book he has been writing and a ministry for him. How far-reaching is the love of God to even reveal His plan for my husband.

Assignment

—— ✦ ——

Tuesday, June 12. Another early morning message convicted me of a sin that I at times shirked off. The sin brought to my attention was the sin of omission. I realized that my neutral and passive unresponsiveness to taking a stand against immoral issues and getting behind my brothers and sisters as they battle societal issues that violate God's Word, was sin. You can't throw your hands up in the air and not get involved in some way. I repented of that sin of omission in several areas and decided I will more actively participate and jump in the trenches with my fellow soldiers of the cross to help in those battles from now on.

Also, I am thankful that the Lord's personal move upon my life has given me more time and a direct reason to motivate me to write and to get back to intercessory prayer. God heard me and answered me. My written testimony is what God has called me to do. This is my assignment from Him. At first I was fearful because of John 3:11. It is where Jesus says, "Verily, verily, I say unto thee, we speak what we do know, and testify that we have seen; and ye receive not our witness."

But whether or not people believe what I write, I will be courageous and boldly declare Him and testify of His work. Will you be strong and courageous and do what the Lord has for you? Over the past several years, I had struggled with writing a book because I was wrestling with the emotions of the material.

At the urging of the Lord to honor this individual I recommitted to go back in time and space to pull the project together. Now I am in the ready again. "Whatever it takes, Lord, to get me where you want me to be" was my prayer. He answered my prayers. Here I am, where I have wanted to be for a long time, and I am trusting Him with what He will do with my life, living by faith in the blood He shed for me.

After I got out of my bedroom, I headed to the kitchen. I felt great. I got my coffee and went upstairs to just write what the Lord showed me. After writing some more, by no means finished, but at a stopping point, I had taken the dogs out for a walk. The temperatures had dropped so much that it was actually cool and refreshing. At one point, I had almost turned back in fear that I wouldn't make it the whole way around my usual route, but at that point of whether to retreat or go forward, the Lord reminded me that I was walking by faith. I went on trusting the Lord.

While I was walking, I noticed many cars parked near the entrance of the gym door. Sure enough, the game was back on, in full swing. I was so happy. A while back, an incident had happened involving one of the players. After that the guys didn't play basketball in the gym Tuesday mornings anymore. This morning all the cars were back. That bad situation must have been resolved as well. Things had resumed to normal there too. Back up and running. Time out was over and the referee blew the whistle. Game on.

After I got back home and came in after such a very refreshing walk with the dogs and prayer time, I fed the dogs. Then I started opening the blinds. As I made my way to the dining room area, I noticed something. The "Laverne" candle that had miraculously continued to stay lit during the past dark days was out. A bit sad but significant that these dark days were over!

I was a little shaky but going forward and trusting the Lord as He directed me back to the office. But the fact that I was able to go back to work made me tear up. Before I got up to the fifth floor to my office, my boss texted me to ask where I was because they had a birthday party planned for me. It was just as sweet as could be. It made me cry as they, including my director, sang the Happy Birthday song to me and gave me a birthday card. After I explained what the doctors said and did and where I was at and what to expect in the upcoming days, we all sat down and ate and shared many funny stories. It was such a nice surprise, and that made it easier to get back into work again. After I got settled back in and as the day went on, I could feel my strength coming back.

Later in the day, I remembered a song which spoke of a man who cried out to God because his soul was vexed with his sin. But the Lord had forgiven him and forgot about it the minute he confessed it. We should have remorse over our sin and weep over it because it breaks God's heart, but we also need to accept His gift of forgiveness. According to Psalms 103:12, which says, "As far as the east is from the west, so far has He removed our transgressions from us."

I believe that this condition that came upon me, specific just to me, not a genetic problem which will not be passed down, but was allowed, appointed, or arranged by God. I am hoping it too will be lifted and diminished into nothing, as if it never happened.

Going Forward

— ❦ —

Wednesday, June 13. Go forward, march onward, Christian soldiers, as the song goes. Just around lunch time Mike and I got back from the doctor's appointment. I am very thankful that at this point it boils down to taking one pill a day. I wouldn't lose my hair and do not need radiation or surgery. I am very thankful and relieved to hear the good news. I can't complain. They will monitor my levels and go from there. My numbers were within 0.3 of being in range. That is a huge relief and big answer to prayer!

During the appointment, while a medical technician was taking my blood, I started telling her how the Lord had been using this in my life. She, being a very strong Christian, told me that we are to be living testimonies. We stopped and looked at each other and knew that was from the Lord for both of us. *Living testimonies.* Living was the word that stuck out to both of us. So if the Lord wants us to be living testimonies, He will keep us alive to testify of His work. The Lord knows when we need encouragement, and He also wants us to choose the high road and keep fighting the good fight of faith. The rays of hope were getting brighter. The reports were getting better.

When I came into my kitchen earlier that morning, the song, "Turn Your Eyes upon Jesus" by Helen Lemmel was playing. Even though I had heard it many times, the message in the song meant more to me now. Also, God brought a message to my attention encouraging us to rise up. My faith will keep me up. Your faith will keep you up too. It is the power of God that raises us up. The Lord reminded me again, that "it is not I that live but He that liveth in me" according to Galatians 2:20.

Broken

We all have breaking points. Some are serious, and some are not so life-threating; but when we get to those points, we have to let go and then let the Lord put us back together. It is hard to be broken, broken utterly, maybe crushed. But if it is the Lord's work, then we need to submit to that and learn what He is trying to teach us. My story is about being broken. Broken is not always a bad thing. Too many people think that they must discard or throw out broken things. That they are no longer useful so just get rid of it. The Lord sees brokenness quite differently. He sees it as an opportunity to heal or mend, to put something or someone back together, better than before, and fit for His service again. Jesus was utterly broken but God raised Him up again. There is hope. In Ezekiel 37:1–14 God told Ezekiel to prophesy to the bones, he did, and God put flesh back on the bones, the breath of life back in them and raised up an exceeding great army of Israel. Jesus raises people from the dead, we have His precious and glorious resurrection power in us!

After I finished eating, I reviewed some notes and decided to press on. I realize that I am no more than a beggar in need of His grace, mercy and touch, but there is hope according to Hebrews 4:15–16,

> For we have not an high priest which
> cannot be touched with the feeling of our
> infirmities; but was in all points tempted
> like as we are, yet without sin. Let us there-
> fore come boldly to the throne of grace,
> that we may obtain mercy and find grace
> to help in time of need.

I turn to Him because without Him, I am helpless and hopeless. I do realize that only Jesus can heal the broken chromosomes in my master stem cell. I pray that He would be the Master of my stem cell—the pattern for all my cells. He is perfect. I pray that He will perfect that which concerneth me according to Psalm 138:8. I hope in 2 Corinthians 12:9, which says, "For My strength is made perfect in weakness that the power of Christ may rest upon me."

Hopefully, one day, when God is finished with me in this time of my life, I will be able to look back and say, "I never would have made it without Him."

Why and How Question

In the waiting time I wondered again, dug deeper, thinking, not only the why but the how question. Was it some environmental hazard I was exposed to that altered my genes, or was it stress? How on earth could two chromosomes just break? Had my sin before a Holy God broken something inside of me and derailed my chromosomes and caused my "wires to get crossed," so to speak? Did I cross a line as a Christian that I shouldn't have? We are to be living sacrifices. We were bought with a price and the blood in our veins, what we do with our life blood, had better not offend His precious blood that was shed for the remission of our sins. I believe that sin could cause a genetic flaw and thus generate deformed cells that endanger the rest of the body, as much as sin in part of the body of Christ can ruin a body of believers. After all, sin is a perverting or twisting of what is good and right. At this realization, my cry was, "God help me!" "God forgive me!" What have I done? Had my sin offended the blood of Jesus and put Jesus in a bad light? Had I misrepresented Him? Sin can cause deformities, even a deformed image of Jesus. God forbid that I go on, or anyone, in any sin before God. Heaven forbid that any of us commit such sin to cause a marred or distorted reflection of Christ.

In the meantime, I asked the Lord to bless the medicine to my body, am very thankful that the treatment is effective, working, and that so far, I am responding positively to it. Maybe, similar to what the doctor said, it is buying me more time until I figure out all that the Lord is wanting to teach me through it. God has been gracious to me and "bought me time" as I understand this and repent of sins He is showing me so that I can testify of His forgiveness, mercy, and grace. I do not want to be like Jacob and live with a limp for the rest of my life. And hopefully this will not be a thorn in my side like Paul endured. Hopefully, the Lord will restore me like Job, after he submitted himself to the Lord's sovereignty and endured extreme loss and suffering. Finally, after Job forgave even his friends, God restored his health and all that was lost in his time of testing, trials, and tribulation. I do know that God is gracious and merciful, quick to forgive and not willing that anyone perish. And I continue to wait on Him and know that he healed the lepers, enabled the lame to walk, gave sight to the blind, and forgives sin.

I felt more than ever that God is ordering my footsteps, and I am obeying for sure. I know beyond a shadow of a doubt that as long as we get right with the good Lord and seek Him first and seek Him diligently, He will make everything in our lives right, including healing a break which is absolutely untouchable by man. He brings order to disorder. There is always hope with the Lord.

Learn to Bow

Thursday, June 14. Courageous faith. We as believers must believe in the supernatural power of God. Interestingly, when I was at the doctor's visit yesterday, my husband and I had to ask the why and the how question. I figured if anyone would have any idea of why or how, it would be the doctor I was scheduled to see that day. An on call doctor who had been a hematologist for over forty years came back out of retirement to assist my doctor in his absence and help out the other doctors in the clinic. He said that he really didn't know why or how this came upon me. But he did say it was as if I was walking down the street and a meteor just came down and "boop," knocked one of my little chromosomes off track. Maybe it was the finger of God; the move of God, maybe it was supernatural, a divine intervention.

Remember in Exodus 4 after God gave Moses his assignment to go back to Egypt? Moses answered Him with "But suppose they will not believe me or listen to my voice." God showed Moses that He could turn the rod into a serpent and back into a rod again. Then God "furthermore" told him to put his hand into his chest and take it out. When he did, it was leprous, white as snow. Then God told Moses to put his hand back into his chest, which Moses did. When he took it out, his hand was restored like the rest of his flesh. If God did this to Moses, it would not be beyond any reason that this sudden break was from the Lord, His divine touch, the finger of God, His mercy to show His ability to heal it as well. Sometimes the Lord might do something in our life to reveal His power and sovereignty to bring us to trust Him more. I am at His mercy. He certainly tested and humbled Job.

We need to bow to the sovereignty of God. I remembered how I had prayed that I would know the sovereignty of God. After teaching a lesson to my Sunday school class on the sovereignty of God, I prayed more earnestly that I would really know it. Now that I am broken, I know and understand and am learning to bow to the sovereign work of God in my life.

They say that life is not for the faint of heart. It is only for the survivor types. We need to be strong and courageous, endure hardship, and have faith to overcome the trials that the good Lord brings to us.

Remember Hebrew 11:1–2, "Now faith is the substance of things hoped for, the evidence of things not seen, for by it the elders obtained a good testimony."

I get it. By faith I am expecting healing and order in the genes of my master stem cell, the substance of what I hope for and the evidence of things not seen (my stem cells can only be seen under a microscope, yet that's where the evidence of my faith can be seen) and that I will obtain a good testimony through all this too. Amen.

As Christians we have to die to ourselves before we can really live for Christ. Earlier I shared that Mike had learned this lesson after a very bad motorcycle accident, that we truly live for Jesus when we are faced with death.

I was feeling good enough to go to work. While I was waiting at a stop light at an intersection which was a block before the building where I work in, before the entrance to the parking garage, I saw something that encouraged me. The license plate on the car in front of me said "Keep Pounding." It was relative to the Carolina Panthers, the NC pro football team, but the words spoke to me to keep going, not to give up until I have the victory.

I have to share one more thing that the Lord did because it shows the far-reaching love of God. I had been praying, hoping for a change in the office I work in for years. I had a feeling that my condition would change the dynamics of the office. Lo and behold, during a staff meeting, my boss told the group that she wanted a clean slate in the office.

She explained the details and even apologized for anything she had said or done that came across the wrong way or hurt anyone. I was very thankful for how the Lord even used my situation to have a "let's put the past behind us and work together" atmosphere. It was huge.

Golden Opportunities, Don't Miss Them

───────── ⟨ℐ⟩ ─────────

F riday, June 15. Have you ever caught yourself? A slip of the tongue in a knee jerk reaction, but really didn't mean what you said. Then you realize that you might have just missed an opportunity to witness to an unbeliever. Before I left the office for the weekend, I went to my boss to wish her a good weekend. I asked her if she had any plans since it was Father's Day weekend. She told me that since her father passed away she didn't have any plans relative to the holiday. But as I turned to leave, I caught myself and realized that I had missed an opportunity to tell her about my Heavenly Father. Either I missed a golden opportunity and need to be more careful to be ready to share my faith at any time or maybe it just wasn't the right time. But as I walked down the steps, I realized that I had given too much time toward being a "man pleaser" rather than a "God pleaser." God has helped me and can help anyone else who turns to Him to be more concerned with pleasing our Father in Heaven, to seize every opportunity and boldly, in love, tell the truth.

Colossians 1:27b, "Christ in you the hope of glory," really gripped me in a new way; Jesus in me, in you, is the hope of His glory. He, in us, His glory in us is what I hope for in life. We want Him to be glorified in us. That is our hope. Without Him in us, there is no hope, no glory to be revealed through us.

There are people out in this world, souls hanging in the balance, who are at their wits' end, "tossed to and fro" according to Ephesians 4:14. Psalm 107:27 says, "They reeled and staggered like a drunken man, and are at their wits' end." They are tired and weary, and we need to bring them to Jesus. Someone in your life was obedient to our Lord's commands and brought you to Jesus. We need to be about rescuing the perishing, about our Father's business.

There is plenty of work to be done. In the upcoming days I will continue to trust the Lord and cherish your prayers as I go forward one day at a time, walking by faith. I have written this to give a testimony of what the Lord has, is doing and will do and how He has moved in my life, showing me truths that I feel compelled to share with you. I hope it is a blessing to you. Thank you again for your love and prayers.

Choices

Sunday, June 17. Two verses my helper and I used for the children were still up on the board of the classroom where we teach Sunday school. First Peter 1:16 says, "You also be holy in all your conduct, because it is written, Be holy, for I the LORD am Holy" (Leviticus 11:44).

Holiness, without sin, is impossible without God. We make many excuses for our conduct, blame it on the devil, or circumstances or weakness. When we start compromising, we drift from absolute truths. Before you know it, you can get way out there, like I was, away from where the Lord wants you. But again, there is always hope in the Lord. If you turn to Him, He will help you just as He helped me. The other verse we left on the board was 1 Corinthians 5:17, which says, "Therefore, if anyone is in Christ, he is a new creation."

Therefore, we can, in our new life as a Christian "Be holy." Often, it is just a matter of our choices. Paul often exhorted us to conduct ourselves aright. Whatever loss we have is gain. Philippians 3:7–10 says, "But what things were gain to me, these I have counted loss for Christ…that I may know Him and the power of His resurrection, and the fellowship of His sufferings, being conformed to His death."

In Matthew 16:25–26, Jesus tells us that if we want to save our life, we must lose it for His sake, then we will find it. According to 2 Timothy 2:3, we are soldiers of the cross and are to "endure hardship as a good soldier of Christ Jesus," and "no one engaged in warfare entangles himself with the affairs of this life, that he may please Him who enlisted him as a soldier."

Tall orders, right? I work for a Commission that issues orders that become law. And there are always protestors. Jesus' commands are all very difficult to achieve and contrary to the world we live in, and yet even the world feels we are waging an unseen war. We, as Christians, when we get serious, according to Philippians 4:13, "can do all things through Christ who strengthens us."

Not until the issue is pushed, do we dig deep. So deep, so past our limits that we break through to the supernatural, to God's Spirit in us, the hope of Glory.

Jesus' Worst Moment Became His Greatest Moment

Monday, June 18. A pastor was talking about Jesus and said that Jesus's worst moment became His greatest moment. I shall say that I can relate to that statement because this diagnosis broke me in a way as never before, and there is no explanation other than it is a God thing. I also know that l will not go on in life without His healing and resurrection power granted to me from our Father in heaven. Have you had one of those worst moments of your life that actually turned out to be a defining moment? Maybe a crossroad or a moment that you made a life changing decision. I have had many but there is an ultimate time where you are at your worst and just have to trust God to get you through the difficulty or challenge and then when it is over and you look back, you know it was totally God.

Time to Get Ready

Thursday, June 21. A wake-up call, especially threatening life, makes you think about getting right with Jesus and ready for His return. We don't know how much time we have, but we have time now to get ready. Now is not time for us or the church to fall away. If salt loses it flavor, and we are the salt of the earth, then how can we impact the world? (referring to Matthew 5:13). The message is that across the board, we must get right and must have a revival in the church. This has been all about what I have been going through. God's people must be broken because of their sin. Again, this is what the break down in me has caused. It caused me to be sorry for my sin, repent and change. I needed a wake-up call. Do you need something to shake you up, shake you free, wake you up? Better to get right now before it is eternally too late.

This is my input; remember the parable of the ten virgins from Matthew 25:1–13? You should read it again or read it if you have never read it. Jesus said that the kingdom of heaven is likened to ten virgins who came out to meet the bridegroom. But only five of them were wise and took their oil in their vessels with their lamps. The other five were foolish and took their lamps but took no oil with them. While the bridegroom was delayed, they all slumbered and slept. Does that sound familiar? Then the midnight cry was heard announcing His coming. Time to gather to meet Him. The ones who had oil refilled their lamps, trimmed their wicks and lit their lamps. It is almost time to trim your lamp. Please hear that. But for the foolish women who didn't have oil: dry, empty without the Holy Spirit in them, they could not light their lamps; and by the time they went to buy some, it was too late; the bridegroom, Jesus had come and taken home the ones who kept their lamps lit, the ones who were ready and waiting for Him, the ones who knew Him and He them. Jesus lastly warned us to watch and pray because we don't know when He is coming back. We just need to be ready.

Blockages

Friday, June 22. There are two big causes of a blockage between you and the Lord and a proper flow of the Spirit: when we quench the Holy Spirit and when we grieve the Holy Spirit. The Holy Spirit reveals Jesus to us. But we can reject Him by quenching His Spirit and by snuffing out His voice. He is gentle and urges us and does not force us to do anything beyond our will. But if we continue to ignore His voice and His leading, eventually His voice becomes fainter and fainter until you don't hear Him anymore; and then you have snuffed Him out of your life. You had better not quench the Holy Spirit because otherwise your light will go out. Don't quench the Holy Spirit and don't grieve the Holy Spirit. This could be likened to blockages in the blood vessels in the body. If the life-giving flow of blood is blocked, it leads to physical death. Thus it is with the Spirit: blockages that restrict the free flow of the Holy Spirit can lead to spiritual death (separation from God). Grieving the Holy Spirit occurs when you, as a Christian, habitually live contrary to, disobey or refuse to do His will. Don't get to a point where you rationalize your sin. The remedy or cure for this is 1 John 1:9, "If we confess our sins, He is faithful and just to forgive us our sins and to cleanse us from all unrighteousness."

Seeing Him Who Is Invisible

⁓

Sunday, June 24. Hebrews 11 is known as the faith chapter. Most Christians think of the first verse of the chapter. However, a point I want to share comes from verses 27–28, which explain the faith of Moses: "By faith he forsook Egypt, not fearing the wrath of the king; for he endured as seeing Him who is invisible. By faith he kept the Passover and the sprinkling of blood, lest He who destroyed the first-born should touch them."

Moses kept God's instructions to him and what was to be implemented and followed by all Israelites, because He knew that God could destroy them as much as He destroyed the Egyptians. We, like Moses, need the fear of God "lest He who destroyed the first-born of Egypt" should touch us. God is good, and He is our healer. But we can't live as we want to, cozying up to the world, justifying sin, making excuses, not walking and choosing to follow the Lord. When Moses was up on Mount Sinai getting the Ten Commandments, the people lost sight of Moses and God, got tired of waiting for him, and began to live in idolatry and practice all sorts of corrupt and immoral behavior. God saw their sin and sent Moses down to deal with His people. God sees us too! I hope that as God's people we never lose sight of Him and His Word in this sin sick world to the point that we compromise or even worse, turn away from what we know we are supposed to be doing and suffer the consequences. All of God's people that chose to live apart from God's laws and ways were killed, and some fell in the crack of the earthquake that swallowed them up. Actually, I am surprised at how many Christians live so worldly. If God treated His own people that way, what makes Christians think they are above the Jews and above God's reproof? Moses kept the Passover, obeyed God and His commandments. He had the fear of God in him. Again, he was mindful of God "lest He who destroyed the first-born should touch them." Moses lived a holy and consecrated life. I live in this world as much as every other Christian. I have a full-time job in commerce and the government. It is hard to live as a Christian, always pleasing the Lord. Recently, one evening, my youngest son came home to help walk his dogs. He had a long day at work and we were talking about the difference of being in full-time ministry versus being a Christian and working a regular job. He thought the hardest was to be in the world but not of the world (see John 17). I agreed. But God has provided what we need to help us, namely the Holy Spirit,

God's Word, prayer, fellowship, attending a good church, Christian radio and Christian television programs. We just need to choose Him. Ephesians 6:10b says, "Be strong in the Lord and in the power of His might."

Zechariah 4:6b says, "Not by my power or strength but by My Spirit, says the Lord."

This evening, I almost decided not to go to church, but I went anyway. Because it was my turn to serve as a nursery hostess, I thought I would go to serve and then come home. But since I was feeling good, I decided to stay and go to the service. Turned out that a missionary from Lima, Peru was visiting. My son-in-law is from Peru. After his introduction and video, his wife and a few of his children got up and sang a song. To my surprise, the words of the song very much encouraged and ministered to me. Some of the words were, "God makes no mistakes" and "When He is done we will come forth as gold." Then I remembered that at the very beginning of this ordeal, a pastor said that gold is only purified went the heat is turned up. I was reassured that this cancer had not been a mistake; and when He is done with me, I will come forth as gold, after the refining process is done.

Full Ownership

Monday, June 25. Owners have rights. Stewards have responsibility. The Father has taken full ownership of us! We are His stewards of what He entrusts to us.

Surrender/Lay It Down

꧁

Tuesday, June 26. Surrender. Why is that so hard to do? There are a few reasons that come to my mind. Don't ever give in to the enemy, even if it is a hostile take-over. Fight. Pride makes us puff ourselves up and not let someone else have the upper hand. Deep down, you think that you are better than someone else, but are you? How about the pecking order in families? Does the oldest sibling always call all the shots or is there a time they have to realize and adapt as time has outgrown their role and changed the family dynamics? We have to be ready for change and at some point, realize, when it is time, train up the next generation and lay down certain areas that we might have excelled in for years and pass the torch. Some of us have been driven to succeed, whipped into shape. You were told over and over to not let anyone else in front of you even if it turned you into a maniac, a participant in road rage. We need to lay our lives down, who we are, and pick up what He wants for us. In James 4:10, God calls you to "Humble yourself in the sight of the Lord, and He shall lift you up."

Appointments with God

꧁

Wednesday, June 27. Appointments with God. Recognize them and never miss them. When God calls you or you sense His leading in your spirit, answer positively and yield to Him. Today I had several appointments. Well, I or anyone else, in their right mind wouldn't think of missing their scheduled appointments, right? The drive or motivation in going to scheduled appointments for anyone is that you wouldn't want to perhaps neglect plans or results of a test that might be crucial to your present or future health, finances, or business. But there might be a deep-down fear of the unknown and in a shortfall of courage you would rather not know what is going on regarding that particular area or situation. You may be wishfully thinking everything is all right, rather than to know the truth before it is too late. Also, you might just need clarification, peace of mind, or hopefully receive the good news that you had been praying and waiting for. God trumps any and everyone else. He is God Almighty, and we would be foolish and sinful to shrug Him off, put Him off or make Him wait or even worse turn away from His calling and leading. Don't miss your appointments with God. God is good all the time.

While I was driving to one of my appointments, a song came on the radio. Most of the words of the song come from Psalms 42, "As the deer pants after water so does my soul longest after you. You alone are my heart's desire and I long to worship You."

Likened to coaching a game, a coach will usually call a time-out when things aren't going well in the game. They huddle, regroup, strategize, rally up and then go back out there to win. Jesus is like our coach and He can call the time-outs in our life for us to refocus and reprioritize before He sends us back out into the world. This time out for me has been from the Lord. In the Bible, there are times too when God's people were facing imminent defeat, they turned to the Lord and rallied around Jehovah. They raised up and sounded the horn of their salvation as they went out to victory. Then God showed or demonstrated His great acts of mercy. Jesus loves us even though we don't deserve it. Many times in the Bible, God's people in battle were outnumbered by the enemy, but God, rich in mercy, fought for them, gave them the victory, gave them the spoils of Egypt, and God was glorified. God came to rescue us from our enemies.

If we saw the numbers, odds stacked against us, the times we failed Him and couldn't keep all His commandments, we would throw in the towel. But it isn't about us; it is about Him. In spite of our shortcomings, He has been so good to us and time and time again demonstrated His mercy toward us. He restores us. Don't miss anything God has planned for you.

Impossible Tasks

⟡

Saturday, June 30. Impossible tasks. Have you ever had one? Amidst our complicated lives, have you ever had a beast of a problem that just crushes you? I do believe that they are allowed by God to break us down to nothing so that He can raise us up and rebuild us His way.

As Mike and I took a walk we came across leaves on the ground. In the heat of summer, several had fallen and they were the color of autumn leaves. I had never seen that before today. We felt that it was a sign that the Fall would be an end to the intense heat of this battle I was in.

New Wineskins

———— ✺ ————

S unday, July 1. Mark 2:18–22. Verse 22 says, "But new wine must be put into new wineskins."

God can make all things new. Don't we all want new beginnings, second chances? I have lost track of the times He has forgiven me, overextended Himself, been longsuffering, not willing that I or anyone should perish, and how He has been faithful to His Word. He isn't going to pour His spirit into the old man but into us as new creations in Christ Jesus. See, Jesus came that we may have life and have it more abundantly.

Open a Window

Monday, July 2. In passing, someone said that we have to shut the door to the world and open a window to heaven. Sometimes we need to put the hand up to the pull of the world system and open up the Word of God and pray.

First Love / Renew a Right Spirit

— ∽ —

Tuesday, July 3. A friend from work gave me two tickets to see *Foreigner* at the Walnut Creek Amphitheater that evening. Since it was blasted hot, she and her husband didn't want to sit out in the heat. Mike and I used to listen to that rock band. So, at first I thought it would be a blast from the past. Many groups my husband and I grew up with are circling back around. Most still sound as good as they did in the seventies and eighties. Turned out that we did not go because of the heat, the crowd, and Mike had to work late. But later that evening Mike and I pulled up some of Foreigner's old songs. Once these songs rocked my soul. But as I listened to them as a Christian, all I hear is emptiness, wrong priorities and wrong focus in the lyrics. It just expressed their lost souls. One of the songs we listened to made me think of Revelation where Jesus wants us to return to our first love to Him. The world can only try to express what they are looking for in a physical or emotional or mental sense. But what they really need is the love of the Lord, the Lover of their souls. People need a passion for Jesus. Horizontal relationships with people will never be fulfilled until the vertical relationship with the Lord is first in your life. Young people hate to hear that, but it is true. For Christians, it is returning to the Lord, our first love. In Revelation 2:4–5, Jesus said,

> "Nevertheless, I have somewhat against thee, because thou hast left thy first love. Remember therefore from whence thou have fallen; and repent and do the first works, or else I will come unto thee quickly and remove they candlestick out of this place, except thou repent."

If you obey Jesus, then the mind, body and emotions will follow.

Have you ever known the love of the Heavenly Father? Do you know what I am talking about? First John 4:19 says, "We love him, because he first loved us."

If you don't know the love of the heavenly Father, then you still need to get born again. In John 3:1–12, a man named Nicodemus that came to Jesus at night. He was a man that I believe inwardly believed Jesus and sought Jesus for the truth. But Nicodemus was a Pharisee, a ruler of the Jews. In John 3:2, Nicodemus says, "For no one can do these signs that You do unless God is with him." In John

3:3, Jesus told him, unless one is born again, he cannot see the kingdom of God. Nicodemus needed to be born of the Spirit. Nicodemus was a wise man. He was seeking something he was missing, and he knew Jesus had it. It was something that goes beyond the flesh; it was spiritual. Jesus explained that he needed to be born again, not of flesh and blood but in the Spirit. In John 3:15–17, Jesus said, "That whoever believes in Him should not perish but have eternal life. For God so loved the world that He gave His only begotten Son, that whoever believes in Him should not perish but have everlasting life. For God did not send His Son into the world to condemn the world, but that the world through Him might be saved." "Whoever," means you, "Him" means Jesus, and "eternal life," does not perish like the flesh, but is spiritual. Only the Lord can give life which lasts forever. Jesus does not condemn us. He did not come to criticize, reprimand, rebuke or give us a death sentence. He came to save us. God so loved the world, even you and me. He really did love us first. He came to us. First John 4:19 says, "We love Him because He first loved us." Having never truly felt loved, I personally had no idea what that meant. It took me a long time to understand certain truths because I had so much worldliness, darkness, void and lies told to me. In John 10:10, Jesus told us, "The thief does not come except to steal, and to kill, and to destroy. I have come that they may have life, and that they may have it more abundantly." God made the first move. He sent, He loves, and He saves. Genesis 1:1–3 is one of my favorite verses: "In the beginning God created the heavens and the earth. The earth was without form, and void; and darkness was on the face of the deep. And the spirit of God was hovering over the face of the waters. Then God said, 'Let there be light'; and there was light." These verses are very comforting because it gives me hope that His Light can extinguish the deepest darkness. Jesus is the light and He can give you a new beginning, a fresh start, a new life in Him. Psalm 51:10-12 says, "Create in me a clean heart, Oh God, and renew a right spirit within me. Cast me not away from thy presence, Oh Lord, and take not thy Holy spirit from me. Restore unto me the joy of thy salvation and uphold me by Thy free Spirit. And renew a right spirit within me." Is this your prayer, is it your hope, a clean heart, forgiven, cleansed from iniquity? If any of this speaks to you, take a moment to pray and ask the Lord to forgive you of your sins, save you and renew a right spirit in you.

Change

────────── ⁓ ──────────

Wednesday, July 4. Independence Day. This morning I took the dogs out for a walk and came across a big feather. It was probably a hawk's feather, but it looked as if it could be a feather from an eagle. Other than being out of place, what caught my eye was that one end of the feather looked new, clean, but the part closest to the end looked fuzzy, like baby hair. I thought about the story of the eagle's molting process. The last phase before the eagle is ready to fly out again is when its feathers are full and mature. When I saw the feather I thought of Isaiah 40:31, which says, "Those who wait on the Lord shall renew their strength, The shall mount up with wings like eagles, They shall run and not grow weary. They shall walk and not faint."

Then I saw a perfect yellow maple leaf. It was a fall color. The leaf was not flawed, no marks on it and it looked very healthy, not dried out. I believe that it was another encouragement from the Lord that the Fall would be when I would be turning over a new leaf so to speak, a new start and change.

Again, the Lord was showing me the fall would be when I would be free and past this disease. As of my last appointment with my hematologist, he said that since I was way ahead of the milestones, he might schedule another bone marrow test in September. That is the true litmus test. Lastly, I came to a part of the field where the grass is perfect, thick and feels like thick carpet with thick padding underneath. Then I noticed that there were dried up dead leaves that blew over the top of the grass. The new grass was completely untouched by it. It was as if the wind just brushed the leaves off the trim, hearty new healthy green lawn.

Yesterday morning Mike showed me a leaf that he had picked up. For real, it was a yellow leaf that had two brown strands, a short one and a long one, unbroken. He said, the chromosomes, they are healed. "Faith is the substance of things hoped for, evidence of things not seen. For by it the elders obtained a good report" (Hebrews 11:1–2). I saved it as a memorial or token, a sign of His work and what is to come. I am excited to see the Lord's work. What change we should really look for is a new start in Him as a Christian. Does God see a change and newness in you that is more like Jesus?

Clutching On or Letting Go

— ❦ —

Saturday, July 7. Are you clutching on to the old or letting it go? This morning it was raining cats and dogs. The house was darker than normal because of the cloud coverage. I noticed the candle on my dining room table that my faithful friend had given to me for the fourth. I had not used it yet. This morning would be a perfect time to light it. So I did. The candlelight illuminated the area and gave off a cinnamon fragrance as it burned. I was glad that I got another candle. I missed the Laverne candle. It was special to me. It was part of the testimony of God's grace. I will remember what the Lord did through those dark days, how He led me, provided for me, saved me, healed me, and blessed me. I do have memorials in my life. Do you? The milestones that mark His work are what I value more than gold and silver. Do I hold on to precious memories, maybe sometimes a little too long? But I am learning to testify of what the Lord has done through them, publish them, and then go on to what the Lord has for me next. We can cherish those special times but not be held captive by them.

We don't want to stunt our progress—progress as pilgrims. God is good, and He gives us more times—times for our good and for His glory. Our times are His. God give us grace to hold on to what He wants us to hold on to and let go of what He wants us to let go of.

Purge

Sunday, July 8. A few truths from the message at church this morning spoke to me, relative to answers to prayers. The passages that my pastor used in his message were from 1 Corinthians 5:7–8 and Exodus 12:1–12. It was in preparation for Holy Communion. The Word that leapt off the page to me was the word, the command, to "purge." Earlier I had touched on 1 Corinthians 5:7: "Purge out therefore the old leaven, that ye may be a new lump."

The old leaven, or sinful man and sin can contaminate the whole lump. Paul was using the example of how a little leaven can leaven the whole lump similar to sin. Even a little sin can infect or contaminate and spread to the whole body. We must nip sin in the bud and realize there are consequences to sin. A former senator and governor once said, "Unless you push a consequence of wrong actions, nothing will change." People wait to come to Jesus until the consequences of wrong choices catch up with them, but don't wait: come to Jesus in love before there are bad consequences. We are commanded to purge or clean out the sin, or leaven, in our lives, which leads to a self-destructing life of malice and wickedness, immorality and evil. Allowing God to purge us of sin is the only way to save the spirit or soul of a man. Chemotherapy is meant to purge the body of all the bad cells so that they don't spread and contaminate the rest of the body. Spiritually speaking, we must purge ourselves from sin so that it does not spread to the rest of the body.

There was another verse that spoke to me relative to my testimony. Exodus 12:13b says, "When I see the blood, I will pass over you, and the plague shall not be upon you to destroy you." This passage comes from the chapter regarding the Passover. God told Moses that the last plague that He was going to bring upon the Pharaoh, the gods of Egypt and the people, was the spirit of death. It would be the final execution of His judgment before the deliverance of His people from the hand of the enemy and from bondage. To protect His people that were in the land of Egypt, they had to get a male lamb without blemish, kill it in the assembly of the congregation, and then take the blood of that lamb and strike it on the two side posts and the upper post of their houses. At the midnight hour, when the Lord would come through the land, He would smite all the first-born, both man and beast. However, when He saw the blood applied, He would pass over them; and the plague would not come upon them to destroy them. The blood of the lamb, significant of the blood of Jesus, would cover them and save them from death. The Blood of the Lamb, Jesus, saves us as did the blood of a spotless lamb covering His people's doorposts saved them from the plague that destroyed the unbelievers.

The last and most important thing that happened to me was the Holy Communion that we observed and participated in that evening. Never had I taken it to heart and related to it as now. Jesus' Body was broken; a part of my body was broken, two strands of my DNA, that if left untreated, could have eventually taken my life. I realize that this is just a smidge of what Jesus suffered. God allowed, arranged and appointed the brokenness that Jesus went through to relate to mankind and pay for our sins and save us for eternity. Jesus was broken for me and for you. This DNA break in my life was His way of breaking me and showing me that only He could repair it. I believe that God allowed, arranged, and appointed this in my life since there was no sure known cause, no inherited flaw and no way to pass it along. His blood was shed for us for the remission of our sins. The price for our sins, wrongs, and offenses was paid with His Blood. His work took care of my sin, my brokenness that only He saw. Only His resurrection power and redemption can restore me back to health and wholeness. It was a Holy Communion that I will never forget.

Roots

Tuesday, July 10. I woke up in the middle of the night. It was as if I could see a root. What are you holding on to? Ephesians 3:17 says, "that Christ may dwell in your hearts through faith; that you, being rooted and grounded in love," This world, the flesh and the devil would like to uproot us. But it is the love of God in our hearts that keeps us. His love is what we are rooted in and His love holds on to us. Jesus is like a root, pulling up fresh, clean water, bringing refreshment, and giving life to the branches in His tree.

The Light

─────── ⌘ ───────

Wednesday, July 11. Josh came with me to my doctor's appointment. Good news was that my numbers had dropped, so they are giving me a break from the chemo. Praise God, I get to back off the medicine until Monday when they will do another blood check. In the meantime, I get to recover. What a relief! I think it was overkill. Too much chemo. Enough is enough! Let God make that decision. Still waiting on Him, because it is not over until He says so.

This morning I saw a picture of a sunrise in New Mexico. The sun was shining through some clouds, even onto a dark storm cloud that was on the right. Whether storm clouds are rolling in or rolling out, the sun is always there. The power of God's sun and light always overpowers the dark clouds of doom and gloom.

Something shiny caught my eye on the side of the road. It was a rock with a lot of mica on it. But it was so pretty and shiny that I put it in my pocket and took it home. The next morning, I noticed it on my countertop.

I had forgotten about it; it did not catch my eye without the light. It takes light to shine. Then I thought about the brilliance it reflected in the light. God might take us out of our dormant place, off the shelf and put us where He can shine on us to reflect His light. The world wants to put us on the back shelf but God can reposition us where we are more effective for Him. Then we can tell people about His marvelous love and salvation.

There are treasures untold, things the LORD shows us that "kings and prophets have desired to see," as Jesus told us in Luke 10:24. We are blessed to be on His paths and to see what the LORD shows us. His paths drip with abundance.

Character

F riday, July 13. Remember the old saying, what won't kill you will make you stronger? We never like to hear that during the difficulty but it is the challenges we face that help us build character. Schools try to build character in children with a list of sixty-six character traits. God wants us to develop Christian character. Romans 5:3 says, "And not only that, but we also glory in tribulations, knowing that tribulation produces perseverance, and perseverance, character, and character, hope."

What tribulation is the Lord using in your life to build Godly character?

Signs of Life

Saturday, July 14. The Lord showed Mike and me something else of what is to come. That day Mike and I went for a bicycle ride in the evening after it started cooling down. We stopped at one of the expansion bridges to look over the Neuse River. He noticed how low the water level was—so low that you could see the bottom of the river. Several big stones and trees that had fallen over along the edges were exposed. One tree was totally down, horizontal on the bottom of the riverbed. I didn't think too much about it until Mike noticed a new stem sprouting a new branch with nice green leaves coming straight up vertically. More encouraging signs of life and answers to prayers!

Good Shepherd

Sunday, July 15. Brenda came home and was eating dinner with Mike down in the dining room. Since I had already eaten, and she had to finish wrapping a present, I was upstairs to finish writing down a few things that the Lord had shown me earlier. Then I got up and looked out the window and thought about the timing, wonder, and miracle of my salvation and the goodness of the Lord. As I looked out into the field, the Lord reminded me that He is a good shepherd and that He takes good care of me and you. I need not worry about anything. Several times I looked at the numbers of my test results and he had told me several times, not to mind the test results, that He was taking care of that too. He really is the good shepherd as He told us in John 10:14. He takes care of His own. Leave the results to Him.

Falling in Place

───────── ∽ ─────────

F riday, July 20. Even if you feel like everything is out of control, you have to trust that your world is not coming apart. Because He is in control, everything is going to fall in place. God is still on the throne, He rules and is orchestrating the events and situations in your life. Continue to trust in the power of His love and continue to wait on Him. Remember Jeremiah 29:11, "For I know the thoughts that I think toward you, saith the LORD, thoughts of peace, and not of evil, to give you an expected end."

Erase

Tuesday, July 24. Erasing the past. We can't erase the past or relive it, but God can forgive it and redeem you and give you a new life; God can make all things new; He can give you a new beginning and a fresh starting point. Jesus said in Revelations 21:5, "Behold, I make all things new."

Wait Patiently

Thursday, July 26. We need to let the Lord have His thorough way, allow Him to finish His work through us and not turn back and miss the blessing. I decided to wait patiently for the Lord. Just so happens that my doctor wanted me to be patient and not rush him.

The other thing happened today while I was walking the dogs. It was hot and sunny but tolerable. I was thinking about the fall. I was really excited to see what the Lord will do, His finished work. Then I looked up and saw a yellowish orange leaf floating down to the ground. God confirmed the fall again. It reminded me of what my doctor wanted me to do—to enjoy my summer and just trust him. I said, "Okay." He is my doctor and he was waiting for me to trust him and let him know that I would trust him. But in my heart and mind I thought I will trust God.

Let Him Watch Out for You

F riday, August 17. At the last appointment the doctor told me to enjoy the summer and let him watch out for me. So I did. I stopped worrying, being anxious and decided to enjoy the rest of the summer. I was glad to see the children going back to school; the days are getting shorter and sensing the tinge of fall in the air.

Why Didn't Anyone Tell Me

— ✑ —

Wednesday, August 22. We were looking forward to starting a new Bible study in the evening. But Mike and I had been running late because we had been out for his Birthday and visited a long-time member who was very sick. I didn't find out until the next morning that the pastor honored me with an award. This whole past year I had been waiting for that moment, and I missed it. I was upset and sad that I missed the service and my one time to shine after twenty years. Frustrated, I couldn't help but think, "Why didn't anyone tell me, why didn't anyone tell me?" I felt so bad. There are no redos. The event happened, is over, gone. Several things crossed my mind that I thought God used to teach me through this and to remember that our true reward is in heaven.

I thought about the 1966 *Peanuts* episode where Linus waits in the cold with Sally for the Great Pumpkin that flies though the air looking to reward the sincerest one with treats. Charlie Brown told Linus that it was make believe. Finally, after waiting all night, it never shows up, and all his hopes are dashed, and Lucy gets upset because she missed trick or treating because she waited for something that never showed up. Linus cries out to the Great Pumpkin, and it never shows up. His hopes were dashed.

I thought about all the children who wait up late Christmas Eve, as I did when I was a child, hoping to see Santa Claus. Actually all I wanted was to see how he fit through our chimney. I remember my parents caught me several years sneaking down the stairs on Christmas Eve and explained that he wouldn't come unless I went back to bed. One year, I must have been about three years old, I got mad because I didn't care so much about the presents as I did seeing him get through the chimney. Eventually I found out that it was just make believe and thought that I was right in thinking that he could never fit down the chimney. I was very much of a prove-it child and I challenged many people and ideas in my life. The land of make believe was never my cup of tea. I didn't have time for fairy tales.

Getting back to the award ceremony, the question of "Why didn't anyone tell me..." resounded in my mind again. The memories of the years of my life in Chicago and New York and Arizona rushed through my mind. I always wondered why no one ever told me about Jesus. I wish I had known Him growing up and many other times in my life. But when I did get saved, God completely changed my life and made everything better. Time and time again as I had thought and prayed about hurtful situations, He told me that He knew. He is the God who sees and understands. We need to tell others about Jesus because there are people in America that still have not heard or have not personally been presented with the gospel and had an opportunity to become born again.

There are plenty of other people out there who still haven't heard the gospel who were like me, lost and they don't even know it. Going forward, with the help of the Lord, I will be more diligent to share the gospel with the people God sends my way. Heaven forbid I miss golden opportunities to share the truth with them. Those are truly the golden opportunities. His blood was not shed in vain. Jesus is the hope to the hopeless like I was. I hope that I can reach the whosoevers in this cold confusing world. So, the question turned to me, as if I could hear others saying, "Why didn't anyone tell me?"

New Normal

Monday, August 27. In the beginning of this a nurse told me that there would be a new normal. I would have to wear a mask due to a low immune system and keep my distance from anyone who was sick. This was way before COVID-19. I would have to pace myself, live at a low level of stress and stay completely positive, and relax. But the Lord used it to keep me from assuming anything and take nothing for granted. The Lord was teaching me to keep shorter accounts and live one day at a time. In Matthew 6:11, in the Lord's prayer, He teaches us to pray that our Heavenly Father will "give us this day our daily bread." Jesus is our bread of life—He is what sustains us daily.

Got It

Tuesday, August 28. I got it. Remembered that we are to live by faith. That is what all these trials are about. This morning the Lord put on my heart to read Hebrews 11 again. I was planning to read Matthew and started there but eventually turned to Hebrews. All the great heroes lived by faith. Yesterday after a friend at work who had gone through a recent hardship and I talked about where we are at, our new normal, living by faith, we took a pensive moment to reflect and wonder. God must put His people in situations where they have to trust God for their lives just like Abraham, Abel, Enoch, Noah, Sarah, Isaac, Jacob, Joseph, Moses, Joshua and many others. Remember Hebrews 11:6 says, "But without faith it is impossible to please Him, for he who comes to God must believe that He is."

God reminded me of something. Not long ago, I had remembered the times this friend and I had gone walking during lunch or a break and how I used to carry cards with God's Word on it. Sometimes I would share verses with her. Then she got breast cancer really bad and we lost touch during her battle. I had missed those walks and sharing God's Word. But God eventually brought her through and has gotten both of us back to catching up here and there and sharing the Word of God, our faith, trust and hope in Him. God's purposes are always meant to teach us lessons and help us through our trials so we can then encourage others and help them through their trials.

Another moment of His intervention happened that I have to share because it is amazing! As I was driving to work, I got caught up in the finances and started stressing about how I was going to afford the bills. I pulled up behind a car at a red light. The wording around the rim of the license plate said, "God's got it." What timing! The Lord orchestrates His work in such amazing ways that He stops the traffic, has this car in front of me with that message, just at the point I was worrying. I am so glad that He is in my life. You need Him too. He is amazing!

Do Your Best

Wednesday, August 29. The next challenge was brought to my attention. I had heard how bad sugar is, but didn't believe it. To me candy and carbs are the best part of eating. Last night I was looking up alternatives to chemotherapy. I read about the Ketogenetic diet and heard testimonies about how cutting out sugar and carbs starved cancer cells. So I changed to more of the suggested Mediterranean diet, to include protein and cut down on sugar and carbs, and included a lot of fruits and vegetables. Hopefully, the removal of sugar/carbs will contribute toward total healing and there will be no presence of leukemia at all. Do your best and He will take care of the rest. Do what you can do and in the meantime, joyfully continue to wait on the Lord. He never lets us down. He is always good.

Placed

———— ✺ ————

Friday, August 31. Haphazardly, I tossed my flip-flops on the floor near my side of the bed. They didn't land exactly where I wanted them to, but I was in a rush and didn't feel like going back to pick them up and straighten them out. I had done that for years and was tired of well doing. I get that from my Dad who was an obsessive neat freak. While I was raising my children, having the shoes around the house positioned neatly was always one of my pet-peeves. We had so many shoes that they just had to be lined up nicely. Plus, rule of thumb is when you take off your shoes you always place them how you would put them on if you had to jump back in them and run out the door. What if there was a fire or crisis and you couldn't find your shoes?

Then God impressed on me that He never haphazardly just tossed anything down. He placed everything exactly where He wanted it to be. The stars and the planets are positioned just perfectly. A degree off could throw the whole universe off. Our work should follow suit. And our words should never be like bullets shooting out of a machine gun. As a Christian our words should be as Proverbs 25:11 says, "A word fitly spoken…is like apples of gold in settings of silver."

According to Proverbs 18:21, "Death and life are in the power of the tongue."

We need to think before we speak. Measure twice, cut once.

Later that morning I heard a true story about a professional football player who was diagnosed with a brain tumor. Until then he was the epitome of health. Why did this happen, how did this happen? I don't know, he did not know, but we know that God used that inoperable and grave condition to turn him to the Lord. Eventually, he surrendered to Christ, repented of his sins and asked the Lord to come in to his life and save him. He came to the same conclusion that I did, that a person isn't ready to live until he is ready to die. It was a reminder that those who seek to keep their lives will lose it and those who lose their lives for Christ will find life. It was a reminder of what and Who we live for, and why, and what our priorities are in light of eternity. Remember all the things that we are blessed to see that God made, He made by His Word and they still are. The moon is still exactly the way He wanted it from the beginning of time. The earth is still in motion. God set it to move in harmony with the other planets. You can rest in

His Word and His work. What He sets in motion is going to come out perfect.

Before the day was over I went on my usual bike ride and I peeked over the side of the bridge. I just smiled as I checked the old fallen tree. Was it placed there for a reason or was I placed there for a reason? Perhaps to remind me of the goodness of the Lord. What markers or memorials has God placed in your life to remind you of His goodness toward you?

See I would have lost hope, "Unless I had believed to see the goodness of the Lord in the land of the living" (Psalm 27:13).

There were even more green sprouts growing up from the dead tree than the last time I had checked, which was another sign of new life emerging, perhaps new areas to grow in and serve Him.

Nothing More Powerful

— ❦ —

Saturday, September 1. Another special morning. While it was still dark, before the sunrise I took the dogs out to the big field. It is always creepy going by the narrow way next to the woods. But Flap, Michael's Great Dane/Black Labrador who lives with us is my guard dog. I trust in God and like Flap by my side too. He is very protective and reactive. He was a rescue dog. If my son, Michael hadn't rescued him, the "dog rescue" organization was going to put him down. They deemed him unredeemable. Michael was his last hope of survival. We prayed for him and helped retrain him. Now he has become the best dog. He is the sweetest and most loyal to us, but very protective and cautious with others. He might have been a hunting dog or a canine service dog. He still is a very big, powerful good watch dog. I felt safe as I proceeded down the dark path next to the woods with him by my side to get to the big open field.

As I got past the narrow trail, it was where I wanted to be, walking in the open field under the moonlight and the stars. After walking the dog around the ballfield, I went to second base, sat down and looked up at the moon and the stars and the midnight sky before the soon coming sunrise. The moon is the faithful witness, according to Psalm 89:37. The light of it glows a soft white light that is so calming and soothing amidst the stars that just twinkle against the dark backdrop of night. Soon the sun peeked over the horizon and appeared so glorious and majestic and strong, ready to run its race across the sky. Nothing was hidden from its powerful light. During the day the sky is so blue, so vast, spacious, free, limitless, untouchable, unable to grasp, incorruptible and without end. The transition to sunset exhibits shades of the blue sky darkening simultaneous to the colorful contrast of brilliant red, orange, and yellow colors against the sky transitioning to midnight blue as the sun sinks below the horizon and the moon comes up and the stars appear again. Words can hardly describe His matchless handiwork. Every day we take for granted the process of our days and nights that God created, implemented and sustains since the first few days of creation. I am glad for His steady hand.

After a morning bicycle ride, I again reflected on the fallen tree at the bottom of the river bank. The green sprouts of new life coming out of the seemingly dead tree still amazes me and encourages me that the power of life is greater than the power of death.

Remember Aaron's rod, a dead stick that budded when placed in The Ark of the Covenant? I thought of the cross that Jesus was crucified on and His blood that soaked into the wood. For a moment, I wish I had the cross that Jesus was crucified on just to have something with His precious blood. But then I realized that the blood of Jesus shed for us is symbolic and spiritual and believing on it transcends time. It is forever applicable to any sin. There is nothing that is more powerful than that truth. It is more than the physical drops of blood, it is spiritual. His blood still provides an atonement and is our sacrifice for whosoever, and still cries, Jesus saves. He fulfilled the will of God. He had to go through the actual crucifixion but there is still power when we apply His blood to our hearts. When someone sins, they have to pay for the sin. Once it is paid, the sin is forgiven. The payment for our sin before God was Jesus's death. He was the sacrificial lamb who paid the price God demanded for our sin. He intervened and laid His life down for us. He took the punishment for our sin. It is over. He did it and the price has been paid in full. If you apply His blood to your sin, you can be forgiven before God. Jesus is our propitiation for sin. He paid what we could not.

The fallen seemingly dead tree at the riverbank that is still bearing new life reminded me of the cross that bore Jesus as He was crucified for your sin and my sin. As I looked for the bottom of the tree that was laying down, I realized that the roots were still in the ground. Even though the actual cross is long gone the roots are still intact. We all have roots or a genealogy to something. The roots of the cross go back to God's plan of salvation and are still alive and true and applicable today. The actual blood on the cross is long gone too but the power of it still saves. Similar to the way I saw new life springing from the dead tree, we have new life from the blood that spilled on the dead tree that Jesus was crucified on. They thought they killed Jesus but three days later He arose. Believing in His death, burial and resurrection and the payment for our sin provides an atonement for our sin and takes us from death to life.

Has your life crossed with the Savior of that Blood-stained tree? Have you come to the cross? This might be your time where you are at a crossroad of life. The real cross is long gone, been laid to rest as it served its purpose. Adam sinned once and all mankind bore the brunt of his sin which is why we are all born with sinful nature. Jesus saved us from our sinful state by His death, burial and resurrection. He paid the price for our sin, and His blood applied to your heart and life can wash away your sin before God. It was done once and for all to redeem all mankind and according to Romans 10:13, "For whosover shall call upon the name of the Lord shall be saved."

Again, the power of that act continues forever and if you apply the blood of Jesus to your sin, you will be forgiven and saved. If you are desperately seeking a new life and want to bury your old life, you can, by praying to and asking the Lord, who has power over life and death, to forgive you for your sin. Ask Him to cover you with His blood and believe in Him to save you and raise you up to a new life in Him. There is always hope in Jesus for a new beginning.

Burn the Ships

Tuesday, September 3. We need to burn the ships. We need to disable any bridge to past sin, failures, mistakes and go forward. Seize the treasures of our trials and conquests and go forward to the upward call of Christ. Don't waver at unbelief. Understand the power of prayer and live with eternity in mind. Be more effective with the years ahead of you rather than looking back at the ones spent. Totally cut any bridge to past sin, failures, and mistakes. We also need to understand the power of prayer and live with the end in mind. We do have a time span and we don't know when it will end, so we had better be about His business. We need to press on in faith and live in God's purpose for our lives.

For sure I am walking by faith, looking for the things that I am hoping for and evidence of things not seen. And I don't go through my days just going through the motions, but I am back to going through the day looking for what God has for me. You should too. All these things will make us live a significant and successful life.

When I was home, in between appointments today, I thought of the importance of perspective. Remember how Joseph and Job kept trusting in the Lord because they kept the big picture of the goodness of God in their minds. They, like Jesus obeyed, focused, waited on God and were eventually elevated to a higher place. Joseph went from prison to a powerful position next to the King, and used by God to save His people during the time of draught; God restored and gave Job more than what he started with, and Jesus was raised from the dead.

I remembered when my mother shared one of two things her mother, my grandmother who lived in The Netherlands, shared before she went home to be with the Lord. Perspective.

Write a Story

Wednesday, September 5. Allow the Lord to use your life to write a story. Could God be using your life to write a story about Him? Be encouraged, it is not about you but about Him, His work, and His love. Amidst the entrapment of the endless day-in-day-out responsibilities God wants to break that cycle and get us to live an extraordinary life for Him. My diagnosis was a break in two chromosomes. Who could have done that but God? This season or state I am in, as the doctor said, "is specific just for you." He told me that there was no rhyme or reason, I didn't catch it, it wasn't genetically inherited and no one will get it and it will not be passed down. It was just specific to me. Because our Father knows what He is doing, I have to believe it was a blessing. He knows how to wield His Sword, He can split hairs, His plan is perfect. No mistakes with God. Blessed be the Lord, He giveth. And I am praying that He will take away. This condition has driven me to discover, develop, and take time for my purpose and gifts in Him. God has given me a unique story about the goodness of the Lord in the land of the living.

We are to reflect Jesus and turn people toward God to be living testimonies. God did not create us to live a stressed out or mundane life. We are created with a unique purpose and need to find that, and live to glorify God.

New Life

Saturday, September 8. Surely He directs our paths. His ways are higher than our ways. Remember when I was explaining the sprouts of new life growing out of the tree that was down? Today when I was on the greenway, I noticed that the dead tree was horizontal, but the new life was vertical! Our old man and flesh (horizontal) is dead, and our new life is in Him (vertical).

A couple of miles down the greenway I stopped for water and noticed a scratch-off lottery ticket. Apparently, someone didn't win. It was probably tossed in disappointment. I shook my head as I thought about whoever that ticket belonged to. There are so many things people put their hope in other than the Lord, that are dead ends, and a waste of time and money. Only God is hope, love and faith.

I rode by a few athletic fields and saw boys playing baseball. Parents were on the sidelines cheering on. One little boy had a NC State Wolfpack shirt on. No doubt his parents were going to make sure he would go to State for college. I remember raising my children. Some parents were gearing their children toward what they wanted for them. I had a family member who spent countless hours playing sports, as I did, for scholarships, and it didn't pay off. You must give your children over to His plan, not your plan for their lives.

There was a track meet on the track/soccer/football field. I noticed how light and unencumbered the young teenagers looked. As the coach was cheering them, Hebrews 12:1–2a came to my mind which says,

> Therefore we also, since we are surrounded by so great a cloud of witnesses, let us lay aside every weight, and the sin which so easily ensnares us, and let us run with endurance the race that is set before us, looking to Jesus, the author and finisher of our faith.

This past Sunday our pastor Emeritus preached in honor of his birthday. He preached from Luke 14 about the Parable of the Wedding Feast. Later that day, while I was riding, my younger brother from New York called to tell me that he was not going to make it to my youngest son's wedding in early November. Before he called, I got wind of it and called him, and left him a message begging him to attend. But he just had excuses. I couldn't change his mind. The situation just drove home the message about the marriage supper of the Lamb and how the people that were invited made up all sorts of excuses not to attend. I just couldn't believe it. I was really hurt and felt so bad as I knew he would miss the gathering of family and friends. My son told me that if the people he invited would not come, then he had a secondary list, to invite others, others that would really want to be there. I guess it was a message that drove home how the excuses caused sorrow because the invited guests turned away from the ultimate invitation to the great marriage supper of the Lamb. But bottom line is that everyone has a free will. He does not force us to come, but we will miss out if we choose not to heed His voice. Why would anyone choose not to accept an invitation to be with The King of kings?

The last thing that came to me that I feel led to share is my thought of a text I sent to my son's fiancé's mom. I shared how excited I was to see her at the upcoming bridal shower that she and her sister were putting together for Heather in Roanoke Rapids. I told her that a few months ago, I didn't even know if I would be at their wedding, but because of the grace of God I would be able to make it to the bridal shower and to their wedding. He is the way maker.

The difference between the grave and grace is the "c" for Christ. He always makes the difference from death to life!

New Beginnings

S unday, September 9. Rosh Hashanah begins. Happy New Year to all my Jewish friends! So thankful for the beginning of the High and Holy days leading to the Day of Atonement, Yom Kippur and The Day of Feasts. Hallelujah to our King of kings and Lord of lords forevermore!

A time of new beginnings, rejoicing, consecration, and repentance.

Rainbow

Wednesday, September 12. I was driving home from work and tired, overwhelmed and worried about several things, especially the upcoming monster hurricane headed toward a direct hit to our coast and path of destruction to our area. The Holy Spirit brought several scriptures to my mind. Then I looked up and saw a rainbow amidst the clouds and wet pavement and just before I went under a bridge the rainbow was right in front of my car. I literally drove right through the end of the rainbow! There was no pot of gold. Better yet, the promises of God. Psalm 19:9–10 says,

> The fear of the LORD is clean, enduring forever: the judgments of the LORD are true and righteous altogether. More to be desired are they than gold, yea, than much fine gold: sweeter also than the honey and the honeycomb. Moreover, by them is thy servant warned: and in keeping of them there is great reward.

It was God's way of getting a hold of me, in His great love and reminding me that He keeps His promises. He is the God of the storm.

Prepare

Thursday, September 14. Be prepared. Be prepared for the coming of the Lord of lords and King of kings.

Brush with Death

Friday, September 15. Another brush with death, as bands of hurricane Florence rage, gnash her teeth at us, beat and whip us, and try to wipe us out as she bears down on our area. God is good and He is greater than even this huge massive storm. Even our Great Dane/Labrador who usually makes himself comfortable on the couch in our living room was scared and wanted to come in our bedroom and get up in our bed all night. But God brought us through another night as the winds howled and the trees swayed and anything loose was tossed and turned. Hey by the way, make sure you, your soul, at the very least is anchored to the Rock, Jesus, to save you so that you are not tossed and turned around by every storm and whim of the world. Ephesian 4:14 says, "That we henceforth be no more children tossed to and fro, and carried about with every wind of doctrine, by the the sleight of men, and cunning craftiness whereby they lie in wait to deceive."

Rather be rooted and grounded in His love, according to Ephesians 3:17–18, 19a which says, "That Christ may dwell in your hearts by faith; that ye, being rooted and grounded in love, may be able to comprehend with all saints what is the breadth, and length, and depth and height and to know the love of Christ."

He hides us in the cleft of the Rock and in the hollow of His hand and under His wing He hides us while the storm passes by, if you belong to Him. If you don't, you have no hope. Hey, this monster of a storm reminds me of the Day of the LORD described in Isaiah 2. Read it. Isaiah 2:10 and 19 says,

> "Enter into the rock and hide in the dust from the terror of the LORD and the glory of His majesty."
>
> "They shall go into the holes of the rocks and into the caves of the earth, from the terror of the LORD and the glory of His majesty, When He arises to shake the earth mightily."

My favorite Bible uses subtitles for sections of chapters. In Revelations 6:12–17 the subtitle is "Sixth Seal: Cosmic Disturbances." It is scary if you have not made Jesus your Savior and Lord. You had better get right with Him before that Day comes, because He cometh soon, sayeth the Lord of Hosts. If you trust in Him you have His promise of eternal life to those who are His, who are trusting in His unfailing love. Psalm 31:6–7 says,

> For this cause everyone one who is godly shall pray to You in a time when You may be found; surely in a flood of great waters they shall not come near him. You are my hiding place; You shall preserve me from trouble; You shall surround me with songs of deliverance. Selah.

Remember the old hymn by Fanny Crosby called, "Hideth My Soul?" It is about a plea for safety in the time of trouble. Some of the lyrics are, "A wonderful Savior is Jesus my Lord… He hideth my soul in the cleft of the Rock… He hideth my life in the depth of His love and covers me there with His hand…and covers me there with His hand… A wonderful Savior is Jesus my Lord, He taketh my burdens away… He holdeth me up and I shall not be moved…he giveth me strength…" The words ministered to my spirit and mind and helped me not be afraid.

Then the rain let up. I thought it would be a good time to take the dogs out for a walk. As I rounded the corner of our house all of a sudden a beautiful yellow butterfly came out of nowhere. It fluttered just in front of me and then it was gone, nowhere in sight. It was a sign from God to encourage me. Storms come and go. Brighter days are coming!

Angels

―――――――――― ✑ ――――――――――

Saturday, September 15. Yesterday, at one point, the wind and rain and gusts really picked up again. The trees outside my study really were looking very unstable. It got very stormy and I had a moment of fear. I started praying again. I cried out to God that He would bring peace to the turmoil. I know that there are angels all around us. According to Psalms 34:7, "The Angel of the LORD encamps all around those who fear Him, And delivers them."

As I wrestled with the flesh and the battle between the visible and invisible, God reminded me again that His Word is true, and I settled myself down and rested in that promise. My next thought was Psalm 122:6, which tells us to "pray for the peace of Jerusalem."

The storm swirling around the area gave me an idea of the turmoil outside Jerusalem with all the attacks of missiles and bullets fired at them by Hezbollah and their enemies, and gave me a real feeling and picture that motivated me to pray for them.

Well, just before I went to sleep I checked Facebook and a dear and Godly friend posted a picture that I had never seen of angels surrounding a believer reading his Bible. The Lord did answer my prayers and showed me a picture of how He surrounds us with His angels.

Good Report

⸙

Tuesday, September 18. Made it to a much antici-
pated very special appointment scheduled for today.
Very anxious for a good report. It is special because a long-
awaited specialized test will be done. Last month my doctor
told me that he wanted to see no more leukemia in this test
result. I was surprised when he said that in a commanding
tone, but I was in total agreement and on board with that
order. I had to bring that to the Lord and continue to pray
for His will.

The past several months have been a lot. God has been
very gracious to me and I am thankful for the care He has
provided and the many, many prayers of so many brothers
and sisters in the Lord. This testimony and good report is
what I owe to you and to the Lord. And heavens, I don't
want to continue to take chemotherapy daily or indefi-
nitely. But there has to be justification not to take it. Today
I am hoping to see evidence of things hoped for and the
substance of things not seen, faith in my healing/cleansing.
I know that I cannot hurry Him. He doesn't always come

when we want Him to, but He is always on time, and in His time, He makes all things beautiful. I continue to be at His mercy. And I know He leadeth me.

I am trusting and believing the Lord for a good report.

This morning was very special. The storm had passed, and the sky was clear. It was just so special as the breeze was lightly blowing out in the open. I decided to just stand there and take it all in rather than go on my usual route with Flap. But he seemed to sense something different too. I decided to go out into the big field where I would see the sunrise better and Flap and I could walk around and continue to enjoy the minutes between the night and the break of a new day and blue skies. It was also special because it is the eve of Yom Kippur, the Day of Atonement. I sent a text to a fellow Christian scheduled for surgery to encourage her from my lowly perspective. I am just a whosoever, but I know the goodness of the Lord in the land of the living (Ps. 27:13).

As the sun started approaching the horizon the light gloriously shone on the few clouds in the eastern part of the sky. It was so magnificent that I decided to sit down on the tarp around home plate. Flap settled down next to me and I started praying as I looked up to behold the glory of the Lord in the heavens. After the sun came up and it was too bright to look at, I got up and told Flap that it was time to go home and eat. Well he just would not budge. I know how he is. If he doesn't move or go in the direction that you want to go, he won't. Even if I pull hard on the spiky collar, I can't move any of his strong 120 pounds. I walked back off the grass and stood on the tarp that covered the home plate. I knew that there was something else that the Lord was going to show me. I looked around and remembered Yom Kippur again and prayed for His atoning Blood to come and wash me and to renew and cleanse my blood. Just one drop of His Blood. I was thinking of His precious Blood that was shed on Calvary for the remission of my sins, I remembered His Body that was broken for mine… was broken for mine. I was humbled and just so thankful for His crimson Blood that flowed, and His Body broken for my sin and yours too. Have you ever had one of those sacred, holy moments where you realize what He has done for you? He was the sacrificial Lamb of God and had mercy on me and forgave me, and His precious Blood shed on Calvary and His Body broken for mine and yours paid the penalty for my sin before Almighty God. I was thankful as I prepared my heart for the Day of Atonement. Then Flap was ready to go because God used him to keep me where He wanted me to be for those few moments in time.

Throughout the rest of the morning and well into the day His Word to me was like surround sound in my spirit. It is as vast as the sky and deeper than the oceans. His presence almost leaves me speechless. There is no better place than in His presence. The sun running its race across the sky is as powerful, strong, high, faithful, bright and warm as His Son in our lives.

God's Timing

——— ⌒⌒ ———

Saturday, September 22. The first day of Fall! Long awaited day this year. One thing you can count on is God's Word and His answers to prayer.

This past Tuesday, the eighteenth, I was disappointed that I didn't have the long-awaited results back from the special tests taken at my doctor's appointment. I had to wait, again. Funny though, I remember that morning a song came on that was about waiting on God's timing. I heard it, but really didn't want to hear it. When I realized that today was the first day of Fall, I remembered the few things the Lord showed me in the heat of the summer, that my healing would be in the Fall. The eighteenth wasn't Fall yet. I would continue to wait on the Lord and learn what He was teaching me in the waiting.

God's healing isn't over, it has just begun.

So I continue to wait on Him cheerfully. Does that ever happen to you, anxious for God to move, anxious to see God's answer but you have to learn to wait on God's timing? God gave me grace to endure and He can to you too. He is in control and knows exactly what He is doing, and I trust in His "unseen" hand and timing. He is the Master of the seasons.

Mike and I are into picking up rocks and stones as we walk along our way as reminders or memorials of something meaningful or special. I remember when I was in elementary school I was a rock collector. Other kids made fun of me because it was boring. I did other things too, but once I shared that, I never told anyone else again. Actually, it wasn't until a few years ago that Mike shared with me that he collected rocks when he was young too. Well, when I was in elementary school, I had gotten a tumbler that took raw rocks and polished them. They would come out at the end of the process totally different than when they were placed in the tumbler. I was fascinated with the process that could take a dirty rock, turn it over and over in that machine and at the end of the process present a completely stunning and smooth rock. Colors came out that weren't seen before and the polished shiny surfaces were always so nice and smooth. The previous rough uninteresting stone became a polished gem. Maybe the circumstances of your life is the tumbler God is using to work off your rough edges and polish you to bring out the special colors He put in you?

When I went up to my study and sat down at my desk, I looked at a stone that Mike picked up sometime this past summer and put on my desk. It is a common stone. Most of it is rough and unpolished, unattractive. At first glance, I didn't want it because it wasn't whole. Part of the stone has been broken off. It always kind of bothered me but I couldn't get rid of it because Mike put it on my desk. This morning I picked it up and I held it up to the penetrating morning sun light coming through my window facing the sunrise. I slowly rotated the stone. Then I noticed the sparkle and shine that the cut surface exhibited. I saw the beauty that the broken part revealed. If the stone hadn't been broken I would have never seen the natural beauty inside that the light reflected.

I encourage you, in your life and in the challenges God is using in your life, to roll with it. Just walk with the Wind, go with the flow of the Holy Spirit's leading. Don't fight the Hands that are holding you. Submit your life to God's anvil of grace and His choice of tools. Let His Light in. In the fiery furnaces He allows in your life, allow Him to fashion and mold you into His image.

Never Push His Work Over

⌗

Monday, September 24. Always seek God and put Him first. Monday morning Mike and I always have work on our minds. But still put God first. This past Saturday morning while I was trying to wrap Heather's present I needed more table space. I pushed Mike's Bible and notebooks back to the edge of the table. It was the only surface I had to work on, so I pushed it over to make room for what I was doing. Later God told me to never push His work over for my work.

He's Still Working on Me

M y doctor had tried calling me on a restricted number, but I didn't pick up because I didn't realize that it was him until the few calls stopped. This morning I called the doctor's office and sure enough, the results came back. The nurse told me that they were very good and that the results were significant. Then she said that the doctor would see me in November. It wasn't quite what I had expected, but it was a good report. I am still not totally leukemia free so maybe there is just a little debris to clean-up like after a storm. The fall season isn't over—it has just begun. My next test will be before the season is over. It's like the leaves on the trees are starting to turn. So, I will be thankful for all that the Lord did. Just at the thought of all this a song came on the radio about holding on and continuing to pray while the Lord works, that encouraged me to forge ahead, not lose heart and to praise the Lord as He continues to work in me.

Learn While Waiting

Tuesday, September 25. Dramatically different and instant is what we always hope for from God. We need to learn lessons from the bad times in our life and not rush God. We just have to joyfully wait on Him, for your time is coming, just wait on Him. After He is finished with us, the "bad" season will be done. But we had better learn from what God has orchestrated, custom made just for our lives, to change us more into His image. Maybe when our lives are cleaned up and free from the debris of sin, others can see Jesus in us more clearly.

The End in Mind

Wednesday, September 26. Significant people live with the end in mind, said a famous preacher. He encouraged us to keep one eye on the clock and one eye on the calculator to make our influence multiply. In what relatively short amount of time we all have here we are to be wise and redeem the time and keep the end in sight.

Surface

Friday, September 28. Mike and I went for a ride down to the greenway which parallels the Neuse River. We noticed that the dam engineers released some water that had been held up at the dam. Since it was after the recent hurricane, it was no wonder there was so much water. As we looked over the suspension bridge, we noticed that the river was past its banks and the water covered that dead tree except for the new branches. What does God want to cover and what does He want to surface in your life?

Be Tenacious

Saturday, September 29. During trials we need to stay surrendered, keep a good attitude and know God's word and His great love. Ephesians 3:1–7 talks of the mystery of Christ and verse 7 says, "According to the gift of the grace of God given to me by the effective working of His power."

Ephesians 3:17–19 says,

> That Christ may dwell in your hearts by faith; that you, being rooted and grounded in love, may be able to comprehend with all the saints what is the width and length and depth and height— to know the love of Christ which passes knowledge; that you may be filled with all the fullness of God.

Have you heard the saying that God is not growing flowers in hot houses but trees in storms? I guess the storms of life force us to dig deep, check what we depend on, wonder what roots us down, what anchors us, what is important to us, what we hold on to, or what holds us when the strong winds test our root system and our sustenance. Be tenacious about your faith. God is on our side.

But God

Sunday, September 30. I understand wanting to work your way to heaven. If you work hard and do good you should go to heaven. If you work hard and do good you should be healed too right? Oh I believe that there is a hell but I don't think I did anything that wrong that I deserve hell. I can give account for my sins and how I responded and changed the direction of my life in the midst of all the wrongs that were done to me. They deserve hell, not me. That was pretty much my Dad's philosophy. One time he told me that he looked for the truth and no one told him. After a bad car accident my mother had, she turned to Jesus and He saved her and healed her of many bad injuries. Doctors told her that even if she recovered from the injuries, the accident set off a disease and there was no hope. But God saved her. My dad saw that her faith in the Lord was real to her and admitted that she had something he wanted, but he struggled with believing in something he could not see. He was a professional engineer and a lawyer, so he really needed to see how things worked and the evidence. He believed that he was dealt a lot of hardship, having been torn from the arms of an illegal immigrant mother, separated from his brother, rejected by his father, and put in an orphanage never to see them again until he was an adult. That was hard. A few years before he died of lung cancer he told me that he would give account to God personally of what he had done. He felt like he had done nothing to deserve hell. Two weeks before he died, after a prayer warrior group from Chicago interceded tearing down strongholds, he surrendered to the Lord and finally accepted Jesus as his Savior.

In church this morning, several people came up to me and told me that I looked good and asked how things were going. I told them of the recent blood tests and results. All good news and progress reports. One lady told me that the chemo I was on was a very strong drug and that I still had a long road ahead of me. Likened to weed killer that kills weeds, it can decipher between the good and bad and only targets and destroys the bad. This new generation drug I am on is specific and there are a few minor side effects, most of which I don't have. So far so good. Whether it is the medicine or God or both, I believe God is at work. The doctor had told me that I was way ahead of the normal milestones. In reality, I am at the mercy of the Lord and so thankful for everyone who has prayed and is praying for me. I could have been dead and gone by now if it wasn't for the Lord hearing so many prayers of friends and family who have beseeched God Almighty on my behalf. No matter how much I diet, follow nutritionist advice, exercise, avoid stress and what I do, I cannot heal myself. I cannot work my way to heaven, there is no payment for my sin that I can afford, I cannot be good enough, I cannot do enough good things to deserve healing or even salvation. It is the mercy and grace of God that will get me through this condition. So, it was a reminder that I can only live in Him. No matter how many good things I do, I am at the mercy of the Lord for salvation and healing.

This afternoon after Mike and I had shared with each other what the Lord had shown us lately, I shared with him that I understand people that buy motorcycles or boats or a vacation at the beach and just want to let their hair down and ride free, be free. Mike and I always liked that New Hampshire license plate that says, "Live free or die." For a moment I felt trapped by this condition. I didn't like taking medicine every day. But then I remembered that it is for my good and I have to believe that God is using it for His glory and my good. Sometimes we don't like the constraint of living as a Christian, but it is out of His great love for us that He restrains us and keeps us from going our own way. Admitting we can't in our own strength and staying submissive and humbled is hard. I think that is one of the reasons some people don't surrender to Christ. I remember one time Mike was in hospital after a bad motorcycle accident. They had to tie him down so he would not pull his cords/tubes out. He got tired of the very things that were keeping him alive, but after I talked sense and truth into him he submitted to the treatment and behaved himself more wisely. Have you ever had a situation likened to that? May 31, Mike shared a prayer. He prayed and said, "Lord, if I can take this cup, let me take it instead of her," and right away God said, "No, this is something she has to walk through." Mike then remembered one office visit when my doctor looked at me and told me that this is "specific to Julie." I didn't catch it, it wasn't passed down and no one will catch it from me. It is just something God preordained or arranged for me. What is your challenge? What is the difficulty you are in? Might it be the very things that the Lord wants to use to do His work in you? Remember Jesus's death on a cross pleased the Father, it was the will of God and it was the greatest act of love for all humanity.

Just after I told Mike that I determined to stay surrendered to Him, I looked up to the right and noticed a smear of blood on the door post I was standing next to. Mike and I looked at it and each other. We don't know where it came from and had never seen it before that moment. It was a sign from the Lord that death will pass me by because my door post is covered with His blood (symbolically speaking).

One more thing—I have merrily been taking my seed, the gospel message and sowing along the North Carolina greenway and have found many responsive souls. The other day the devil threw up a deterrent but God helped me to overcome that obstacle. Snakes are on the trail. They are mostly out to sun themselves or cross the path to get to the river side. The other day I came flying down a hill toward a bridge. I looked ahead and saw a man frozen in his tracks and wondered why. Just before riding over the bridge which he was on, I looked down and saw the biggest copperhead snake I have ever seen. Usually there are black or green non-venomous snakes, the harmless ones. I only had a fraction of a second to make a decision to try to go behind the snake, ride over it or go in front of it. It was too long to go behind it without hitting the railing of the bridge or God forbid, skidding-out and falling on the snake; if I rode over the bridge and missed his head he could rear back and bite my leg and the thought of hitting the snake made me shiver. What if his head got stuck in my spokes and the whole snake got tangled up in my bike? I decided to get the wheel right in front of his head. I figured my speed would be to my advantage. By the way, the reason I didn't veer off the path was because there was a relatively steep drop off on either side of the path and marshy water under the bridge. Stopping was not an option because I was going too fast. With no other alternative I just raised up my feet and screamed "Jesus!" through my narrow escape. I whizzed by the stunned and speechless man and snake and caught my breath. As I looked back, the man and the snake were frozen. God does that—He freezes our enemies before they can bite us. I literally cried a sigh of relief. God is good.

The intricate handiwork of God is so amazing. He creates huge massive things like the sun and the moon and big lions, and yet can minister, touch or move upon us on a cellular or microscopic level.

Yesterday UNC posted the results of the special blood tests. It showed that on September 19, one was completely negative, no presence of leukemia and the other showed only .0622% of every 100,000 cells in my blood still needed to be cleaned out. Good thing is according to the report, they don't start counting until there is a 0.10%. Compared to the June 4 results of 33.875 % of every 100,000 cells were "bad," my results were categorized as scientifically "significant" and "ten times better than expected." That is an answer to so many prayers. I see "the evidence of things hoped for and the substance of things unseen… for by it the elders obtained a good testimony" according to Hebrews 11:1–2. Our faith, how precious it is and our hope is in Him always and forever.

Psalms 71:14–16, "But I will hope continually, and will praise You yet more and more. My mouth shall tell of Your righteousness and Your salvation all the day. For I do not know their limits. I will go on in the strength of the Lord GOD and I will make mention of Your righteousness of Yours only."

This is an ending to a chapter in my life and the beginning of a closer walk with Him. As a nurse told me, it is a new normal. I hope that all that I have shared ministers to you. My testimony is to glorify Him who saved me, and for you to see the answers to prayers, His grace and His love. If you just picked this up and had no idea what I went through this past season, I hope some of the things I shared with you will help you trust in the Lord with your life and help you draw closer to Him.

This morning a very godly lady at church who is known for saying "love you bunches," told me something after she listened to me that sums it all up. She said, "He's got it covered!"

The other evening, Mike and I took Oscar for a walk and we walked by a very tall mature pine tree that surprisingly split and broke off. I wondered if lighting hit it. But Mike said that it was wind from the other nights storm. I was reminded of times I have seen trees weather the storms that have come. Some trees make it through the storm, but some do not. These tall pines can bend in the adverse winds like we can bend in the winds of adversity in our stand as Christians. But at one point if the wind is too strong or comes with too much force it can make a weak or brittle tree snap. If we do not hide ourselves in Christ and we take too much adversity on ourselves, a weak spot could become a breaking point. Beware that you do not leave yourself vulnerable amidst the elements of the world. Be careful to stay guarded, in fellowship, and in His Word.

Too many Christians don't take the LORD our GOD and His commandments seriously. I used to, but then just got too comfortable. I fell into the pot of lukewarm Christians and chose what to obey and what not to obey. I started brushing Him off. Got caught up in the American dream and not the will of God. Where are you?

God and His work is serious and needs to be obeyed. Unbeknownst to me, something in my body had snapped, and was broken inside and I didn't even know. The most concerning and alarming thing to me was that if I died, I was not ready to go before the Lord. I was saved but knew there was so much more I needed to do. Are you doing the work that the Lord has preordained for your life?

One message that I know that needs to be preached through this episode in my life is the fear of the LORD. It is all too easy to let that fade away in this dark and chaotic world. Deuteronomy 31:12 says, "That they may learn to fear the LORD." Hebrews 11:7 says, "By faith Noah, being divinely warned of things not yet seen, moved with godly fear."

God has been gracious, and we all have been given time. We need to use it wisely and do the will of the LORD for our lives.

In the waiting, be faithful. Don't be like the Israelites who turned away from the LORD. Seek and find the will of the LORD for your life and do it before it is too late. He really is coming soon.

This is my testimony of how leukemia was overcome in my life by the blood of the Lamb and the Word of my testimony according to Revelation 12:11.

Be encouraged, according to James 5:11, "Indeed we count them blessed who endure. You have heard of the perseverance of Job and see the end intended by the Lord— the Lord is very compassionate and merciful." NKJV (The MacArthurs Study Bible, Thomas Nelson Bibles Copyright 1997 by Word Publishing). The other evening, I came across an interview of Dr. David Jeremiah and to my surprise he was explaining how he had Leukemia and what treatment he went through. He also explained that he has been fine ever since they did a stem cell transplant. I have not had a stem cell transplant, but this morning God revealed a great truth to me that I must share with you all who have been led to read my testimony.

When we get saved we trust in the blood of Jesus to redeem our lives, save us from sin and death, and to give us new life in Him. And we ought to live in and for Him from that day onward. We are believers in this eternal truth, and we live by faith in the Son of God, Jesus Christ, the Word of God. David Jeremiah's body was diseased, sick, not right, but the transplant saved his life, and undoubtedly many prayers were offered up for his healing as well. The master stem cell that went bad had to be replaced. We are all the same way. We are wretched, unsalvageable, dirty, sinful, destined to eternal darkness, without hope until and unless we trust in the shed blood on Calvary to save us, to give us new birth. We are born again. The stem cell transplant physically gave David Jeremiah his life back. See, the master stem cell is where our life's blood flows from and if it is bad we will die. I have always trusted in salvation through Jesus, but sometimes I want to see evidence of things hoped for and the substance of things not seen. I have asked the Lord to come into my heart, cleanse me from all iniquity and make me whole. Just as I hope in His blood to save me, I need Him to be Master of my stem cell. Just as blood cells are patterned after the master stem cell, so we are to be patterned after Him.

So, the good report is a cytogenetic test revealed a normal pattern in my genetic structure meaning, no more broken strands. My oncologist said that I am in deep, deep, deep remission. God's healing is being revealed, and is scientifically evident. I don't want to be a poster child of this new drug. I want to be a poster child of God's work. So

God is turning the tables and that is what I want: that God will get the Glory for His work in my life. It is His shed blood on Calvary, the fountain of His blood that gives me new life.

This testimony just reveals my weakness and His strength. If He saves you, He is faithful and just to forgive you, and He will regenerate you.

Looking Back

Early in the morning while I was getting ready for the day, Mike changed the radio to a local Christian station and a song came on "Gracefully broken"—that was how the Lord moved upon my life through the broken chromosomes and how God changed my life through it. He is so good!

On Assignment

This was so on my mind: on assignment, on assignment.

Two days later I read an article regarding another Christian that had gone through cancer. She felt like it was her assignment from the Lord. God used it in her life to bring Glory to Himself. Are you doing what the Lord called you to do and what He commanded you to do? Putting all things aside, are you loving Him with all your heart, mind, soul and strength? Are you on point? Are you on His assignment?

The Move

Final touches had to be done on my testimony. I had to finish and relay the messages that the Lord wanted me to show you. After I got back up on my feet with consistent good numbers, cancer was in remission, my strength was back and feeling good, came another test. My husband called me at the office on Thursday and told me that he had just sold our house! Most men see business transactions and make decisions that are best without feelings. He didn't realize what this meant to me. He was trying to protect me from further stress and emotional trauma. The first move involved downsizing and sorting through thirty plus years of stuff Mike and I accumulated and dragged with us since before we got married. The second move into our new home involved a lot of decisions for remodeling on a tight schedule. It was all very stressful, but we continued to pray through it. It all took more time away from finishing my testimony on top of a book he was writing as well. The delay of the move was for a reason. It reminded me that as I downsized we can't take everything with us. Things are things and the uproot reminded me that this earth is not our home. We are pilgrims on our journey to our heavenly home and it made it easier to allow Him to plant us where He wanted us to bloom next. But this fall, after I was declared in remission and thought I had learned my lesson, it started with another break that humbled me again and taught me more that I would like to share with you. Inside I had been fretting. How was I ever going to get His work done? Amidst the bustle, one thing after another, inside I was fretting, as I continued to slide farther and farther away from His work. I had about finished this book called, *Broken*. It is my testimony of overcoming cancer, which a year ago God impressed on me to write in the fall season last year. I was in remission last fall, but let me share something else that happened this fall.

The Fall

—— ✑ ——

The Fall sent shockwaves of pain through my body. The blow took away my breath. It happened so fast. I slipped, I was falling, with nothing I could hold on to. My momentum hurled me up in the air. Once airborne, I came to the awful realization that I couldn't catch myself. Suddenly everything around me turned into slow motion as the room seemed to spin. It wasn't going to be good. It felt like the force of my body weight was all of a half-ton crashing down on the steps. The blow hit so hard that it instantly sent shockwaves of pain and trauma through by body as I landed on the steps. My back broke the fall.

Within a minute, I had to decide whether to stay there or get up. Reasoning out what to do, either choice could make the damage worse. But after a moment of silence, I decided to get up, thinking that the steps and concrete floor were hard, uncomfortable and what if no one found me until hours later. Depending on the injury, even if it made it worse, I wasn't going to die on the steps and garage floor. No way, especially after overcoming cancer and the ordeal of moving, downsizing, and remodeling while continuing to work full-time. When I realized that I couldn't breathe, a burst of adrenaline kicked in, I got up and then called for help. Mike and Joshua were outside with the roofing guys, so it was a miracle that they heard me calling for help.

What in the world? Mike and Josh looked at me wincing in pain, stammering about not knowing what to do. I could hardly spit out a word or catch my breath. I was fighting hard not to pass out as stars clouded my vision. I could hardly stand but I knew if I went down again, I wasn't going to be able to get up again. My back left side and my ribs hurt so much.

When I was up in the air, I was so mad at myself for that one time I didn't put on my shoes. My socks just slipped off the smooth wooden steps. I suppose my speed, and weight thrust me farther than I realized. Anyone who knows me knows that I always move fast, walk at a good clip, and with force. There is a lot to do and I have to keep moving from one thing to another. After sailing up in the air, I came down on the steps. There was nothing to hold on to, so my middle back took the initial blow, then my left side, lower back, and upper back, my left forearm and right elbow and wrist.

I knew I only had a few moments to get help. I struggled to keep myself up and from passing out. Then Mike and Josh said that I needed to go to the emergency room, but I said, "No." Ambulance rides are way too expensive. But I did agree to go to a nearby urgent care. I could hardly stand getting in the car, the drive and getting out. Mike dragged me in to the front desk. Everyone who saw me tried to help me. After about twenty minutes, the urgent care didn't know what to do with me. The doctor's touch under my ribs hurt so much, they were worried about broken ribs, ruptured spleen, internal bleeding and a spinal cord injury. What in the world. I finally could tell them what happened. I was running into the garage to get some measurements of a bed that we were going to put in the study, but my foot just slipped out from under me on the last step going into the garage, and my momentum sent me flying up in the air, only to come crashing down on my back.

Back in Urgent Care, the ambulance was right on it and as the EMS group came into the urgent care they worried about possible life-threatening injuries. The urgent care doctor had called for an ambulance to take me to the nearby ER. I was impressed with their service and felt comforted as they gently lifted me and positioned me just right. No one had ever carried me, and I didn't think anyone could carry me. I finally stopped fighting the, "I can't afford this" thoughts, realizing I just couldn't on my own, I really needed help. It is a terrible place to be at. Once on board, it did take some time to get IV started and a port on the other hand. Usually my veins are very big, but for some reason they seemed to shrink down to nothing, so it took several tries to get it started. They strapped me in like I was going to the moon. Actually, as they all were looking down at me with their blue suits and the bags swaying around, it reminded me of the inside of a space craft.

When we arrived at the emergency room, they all were ready and waiting for me and started the triage process. The big thing was the CT scan which would check for internal bleeding, organ condition and bones. That was another "help me, Jesus" procedure.

They first took off my necklace with my cross. I didn't like that at all. Mike gave me the necklace a long time ago and I never take it off. The cross defines my life. I wear it proudly as it is always a reminder of what Christ Jesus has done for me and who I belong to. Then they rolled me down the halls so fast the ceiling lights seemed like a blur. The dye and the cylinder wasn't too bad but the cold, hard unforgiving flat surface they moved me to was unbearable. The command to put my arms above my head made me feel more vulnerable. They wouldn't let Mike come back to the X-ray lab.

I didn't like being alone and had a momentary flash of Jesus on the Cross. Some hard spots you go through, it is just you and God. But He never leaves us. I had no choice but to grit and bear it. I knew that they needed to see inside before they could make a determination of what to do.

Thankfully after about twenty minutes the results came back. No collapsed lung, the spleen was intact, and there was no internal bleeding. But my back was broken in two places. They said that if it was less than an inch closer to the spine, I would have been paralyzed! With that statement there was a complete silence in the room.

Then everyone took a sigh of relief. Even though I was in a lot of pain, Mike and I and the doctors and nurses were all thankful and told me to be thankful. We knew the Lord was watching over me and prevented and spared me from a worse injury.

They gave me some medicine for pain, but the ride home from the hospital after I was discharged was excruciating. The fall had shifted my pelvis so there was nerve damage, bruising, the severely pulled and strained muscles in my back, the back of my ribs hurt and my elbow swelled up and turned black and blue. Every bump, turn and stop and go shot waves of pain making it hard to breathe. It was almost too much pain to bear. It didn't seem right for me to leave the hospital, but they were concerned that in my weakened state, I might catch the flu that was running rampant. Also, the ER doctor explained that there was nothing else he could do. This was a break that only time could heal.

The next week was so grueling with pain and sleep deprivation that I just wanted to die. I was still assessing the damages and unable to move, couldn't get in or out of a recliner without excruciating pain, could barely walk and could barely talk. I thought about going back to the hospital but didn't know how to do that without an ambulance. It was a rough road and the nights were so dark and so long as I couldn't find a pain free position. In the long darkness, I questioned whether or not I could walk and if I would be stuck like this the rest of my life. Normally I play basketball, regularly bike ride on the greenway, walk the dogs and stay very active. But at this point in my life Mike had to help me move just a smidge every twenty minutes to find a less painful position. He was as exhausted as I was, if not more. But there was hope on the horizon. Word got out and my church and family started praying. There just had to be a turn for the better.

I sought the Lord, "What, Lord?" He had my undivided attention. He showed me that when we, as Christians slip and fall away from Him and what He has for us and where He has us, it causes excruciating pain throughout His Body. God blessed me to feel His pain, and how the error of my ways, maybe your ways, cause Him pain. He impressed me to share this with all His people. One dark and long sleepless and painful night, the Lord told me that many Christians are falling away. When we slip and fall out of what we know to be right with the Lord, it causes others to hurt and jeopardizes our witness. We need to be genuine, truthful, upright and blameless. We have to be mindful that the Lord sees when we disobey. Don't shirk off even little sins, and keep close accounts with the Lord. We as Christians need to appreciate what Christ did for us and never lose sight of The Cross. Too many Christians, without realizing it, commit idolatry, half-heartedly serve Him, do their own thing, have bad attitudes, complain, not giving thanks in all things, blame God, satisfy the lusts of the flesh, compromise, are untruthful and are not worthy to be called Christians. We need to change because the Lord is coming soon, and we can't live as if it will never happen. We can't ever win over unbelievers when they see through us not being genuine. We will be accountable for our lives, time, choices we make and how we relate and communicate to others. I asked God to forgive me for slipping out of place, falling out on Him in some areas and that I was sorry for the pain that I caused Him and His body.

It also gave me an opportunity to understand others who had fallen and couldn't get up, who had trouble walking, the shut-ins and elderly. It made me realize the suffering that others experienced, and I repented of being cold, uncaring and unsympathetic. During the long painful sleepless nights, I thought more of the intense suffering of Jesus during His passion week and the time He suffered on the cross for me. God reminded me that you and I were bought with a painfully high price and I saw the need to be more in line with how I was supposed to live for Him. God used the diagnosis of leukemia a year ago to show me the importance of His blood that was shed for us. God used the break for me to relate to how His Body was broken for us. Now I am at the point where every step I take is in the name of Jesus and now I literally continue to live by faith in the Son of God and in His powerful Name.

Several days out, two ladies from church came to visit me and brought me a few necessary items and food. That was God's love in action! Then the fifth day out I seemed to really be on the mend. The love for me made me feel better. The Bible says that His love covers a multitude of sins. The outpouring from His people with visits, meals, food, phone calls and texts were all out of His great love. It just amazed me. When I couldn't come to Him, He came to me. Our church has been like His hands and feet to me. One day a few ladies came to visit with more meals and flowers. One lady came with a dozen roses which were actually given to the missionary family we honored. But the wife of that missionary heard about my accident and wanted me to have them. Such love could only be the love of the Lord. Jesus, my Lord, King of kings chose to completely surrender His life to God as He hung on the cross to pay for our sin debt we owed before our Heavenly Father

Who, after the payment was settled, would raise Him up again to Glory. The fall humbled me. It made me open up my heart and home to whoever God would send my way to help me. God unlocked and opened the door to my heart and my home. I was always afraid if anyone ever came into my life and home, they wouldn't love me and be critical and not like me anymore. So this outpouring of unconditional love tore down that "high thing that exalted itself against the knowledge of God" according to 2 Corinthians 10:5.

And as my sisters in the Lord poured into my home it was God's love coming in. First John 4:18 says, "There is no fear in love; but perfect love casteth out fear."

The church, His body, my sisters in Christ came to me in His name and loved me with the love of the Lord at my worst and broken condition. They loved me with the love of the Lord. As the days went by, I was so glad that this happened. According to Romans 8:28, "And we know that all things work together for good for them that love God, to them who are called according to His purpose."

Also, 2 Corinthians 4:17 says, "For our light affliction, which is for a moment, worketh for us a far more exceeding eternal weight of glory."

God's divine love overwhelmed me. Who am I? I asked myself. The love of God to me is still a mystery and a wonder.

That Friday, I call my "Good Friday," because it was early that morning when in the stillness of the dark and quiet morning, I took a cracker, put it in my mouth and gently bore down on it. It was in that solemn moment, just at the point when the cracker broke, that the Lord told me that His Body was broken for me. It was a communion that I will never forget. I understood the why. The break was not about me, but about Him and what He did for me and what He did for you.

Epilogue

M onday was the first day of fall. In Matthew 26:6 Mary knew Jesus and understood what He had to go through, so she broke the top off her precious alabaster jar and poured her costly oil on Jesus's feet. We have to allow the Lord to break us and willingly pour out what is precious in us for others. It is what's inside us that is so precious. Jesus was the most precious possession that our Heavenly Father had, and yet He loved us so much that He gave His own Son to be broken, His Body and Blood shed on Calvary, poured out for the remission of our sins so that we can be forgiven and made whole.

A few years ago, a friend of mine was actually hit by a car downtown. She was sent to the same hospital and doctor that took care of my husband a little over ten years ago after a bad motorcycle accident. My husband witnessed to him a lot, but he did not ever change. Then my friend ends up witnessing to the same doctor after her accident. He is Jewish. But he hadn't surrendered yet and accepted Jesus as his Messiah and his Savior from sin. I told my friend to ask the doctor how many more people does God have to break and send to him for him to receive Jesus as his Savior and Lord?

This same friend told me that the other day she stopped by a store on the way to see me. She would have never stopped at that store at that time. She witnessed to a lady there and told her that if I wouldn't have been broken, she would have never come to her. She continued to explain to this lady that God loved her so much that someone was broken for her and she was sent to cross her path to tell her that God loved her so much that He arranged that time and that divine appointment in her life for her to get saved. She did give her life to the Lord! There is something about being broken for Him. Jesus was broken and his life's blood was poured out for us. That is just how much our Heavenly Father loves us and wants us to be reconciled to Him through His Son Jesus and His work in His death, burial and resurrection.

The Lord told me in a very sorrowful tone that many of His people were falling, falling into sin, slipping away from Him. So I knew that was the Lord speaking to me and He impressed on me to pray for His people in these trying times we live in.

The next day, I was reminded that I could boldly approach His throne of grace for help in time of need for

He can sympathize with our weaknesses as Hebrews 4:15–16 says,

> For we have not an High Priest which cannot be touched with the feeling of our infirmities, but was in all points tempted as we are, yet without sin. Let us therefore come boldly unto the throne of grace, that we may obtain mercy to help in time of need.

Also, it's not me but Him. Zechariah 4:6 says, "Not by might, not by power, but by My Spirit, saith the LORD of hosts."

Lastly, the Lord reminded me that He is the potter and I am the vessel, and He can break me and remake me more into His image for His glory. He gracefully broke me and gracefully put me back together again.

Twice-broken, I write this testimony to encourage those who have been, are, or will be broken. There is no shame in being broken. The Master, broken Himself for us, stands ready to pick up the pieces and wonderfully put us back together, stronger and better than ever, vessels ready for His use and service. When the Shepherd breaks the leg of a wandering lamb, it is said that the lamb does not wander again, but stays close to the Shepherd. That's what I call "Beautifully Broken."

About the Author

The author, Julie G. Kennedy is a passionate, born-again Christian wife and mother of three. Born in LaGrange, IL, a suburb of Chicago, she grew up in Scarsdale, an affluential suburb of New York City with two brothers. The middle child of a successful New York attorney and a Godly nurse and sculptor, Julie thought she had it all—that is, until she met God. After graduating High School, she earned her private pilot's license while studying Aeronautical Science at Embry-Riddle, before earning a BS in Business Administration at LeTourneau University in Longview, TX. While at LeTourneau, Julie had an encounter with God that would change her life forever.

She married and moved to Pittsburgh, PA, starting a family of her own. Her husband, an IT Professional, through a job change brought them to the Sunny South and Bible Belt, to Raleigh, NC, where she continued growing in the Lord, through Bible studies, teaching Sunday School, and other Christian activities. Julie has a real heart for young people, and has brought many children to the

Lord and helped them in their walk with the Lord. After working for the State of North Carolina for over twenty years, she is ready to step out in faith, to whatever the Lord has next. Little did she know, but God had another encounter planned that would shake the very bedrock of her faith, but afterwards, would bring her closer to the Lord, on a whole new dimension. Julie humbly gives God all the Glory and accolades for whatever successes and failures He has brought into her life. She is transparent and personal in sharing her faith to bring others to faith and belief in God. She is a prayer warrior, interceding for others to find and pursue God's will for their life. It is not about herself, but all about what God is doing. God is calling her out from behind the scenes to a more public ministry, venturing out after years in a successful career, family, and teaching children, to open the door to her life and in being transparent, to share a glimpse of how God gently picks up the "Broken" and puts them back together His way, and gives a new calling—for "such a time as this."

Currently, Julie lives in Raleigh, NC, with her husband Mike, her two sons, daughter, son-in-law and daughter-in-law. She is still working full time. In her free time she loves writing, drinking fresh hot coffee, going on long bike rides, home improvement projects, playing basketball and listening to Christian music.